BURGESS LEA PRESS

BLP

ALL PROFITS to GOOD CAUSES

BURGESS LEA PRESS
donates 100 percent
of our after-tax profits
to food-related causes.
This book benefits
Wholesome Wave,
www.wholesomewave.org.

DULCE de LECHE

DULCE de LECHE

Josephine
Caminos Oría

Quarto is the authority on a wide range of topics.

Quarto educates, entertains and enriches the lives of
our readers—enthusiasts and lovers of hands-on living.

www.quartoknows.com

First published in 2017 by Burgess Lea Press, an imprint of The Quarto Group, 401 Second
Avenue North, Suite 310, Minneapolis, MN 55401 USA.

Telephone: (612) 344-8100

Fax: (612) 344-8692

quartoknows.com

Visit our blogs at quartoknows.com

Burgess Lea Press titles are also available at discount for retail, wholesale, promotional,
and bulk purchase. For details, contact the Special Sales Manager by email at
specialsales@quarto.com or by mail at The Quarto Group, Attn: Special Sales Manager,
401 Second Avenue North, Suite 310, Minneapolis, MN 55401 USA.

10 9 8 7 6 5 4 3 2

ISBN 978-0-9972113-2-0
Library of Congress Control Number: 2016952742

Illustration Kate Forrester
Art direction Ken Newbaker
Production Victor Cataldo
Editor Diane Abrams

Photograph page 5 property of the author
Photograph page 192 copyright ©2017 Duane Rieder

Burgess Lea Press donates 100% of after-tax publishing profits on each book to culinary
education, feeding the hungry, farmland preservation and other food-related causes.

Printed in China

I DEDICATE
THIS BOOK
TO THE WOMEN IN MY LIFE

First and foremost, my grandmother, María Dora Germain, or Dorita as she was affectionately known, who taught me love through cooking and whose care and dedication continue to shape the woman I am today; my mom, Beatriz Germain Caminos, or Poupée as everyone knew her, my good luck charm who had the grace of making every person she loved feel as if they were her favorite (I'm pretty sure it was me!); my sisters, Verónica, Corina and Barbara, my best friends; and my daughter, Poupée. These women give me the might to move forward every day.

CONTENTS

EN LA MERIENDA
(AT AFTERNOON TEA OR COFFEE)

EN LA PICADA
(ON SMALL PLATES)

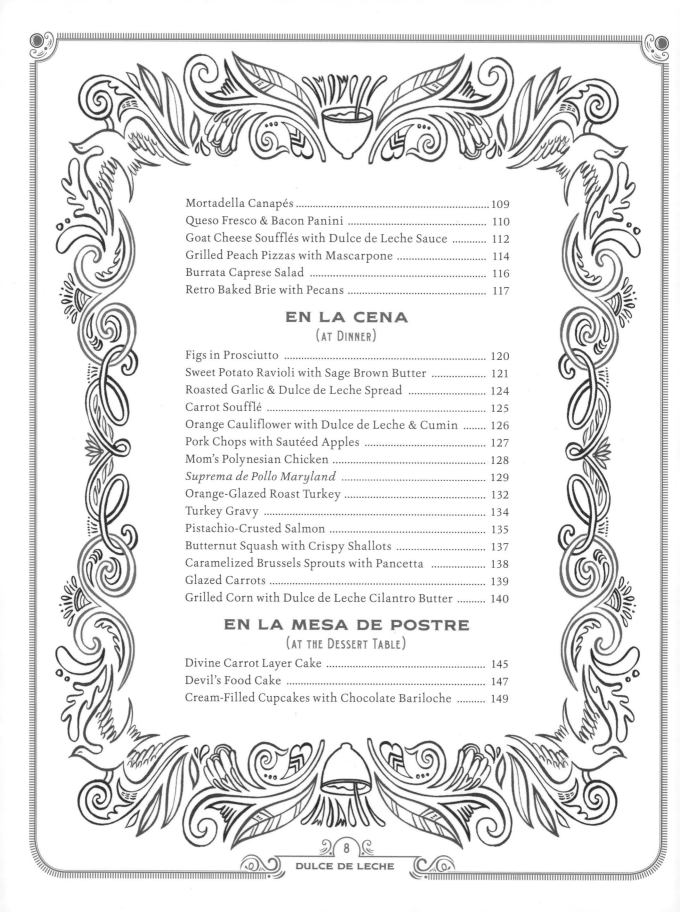

EN LA CENA
(AT DINNER)

EN LA MESA DE POSTRE
(AT THE DESSERT TABLE)

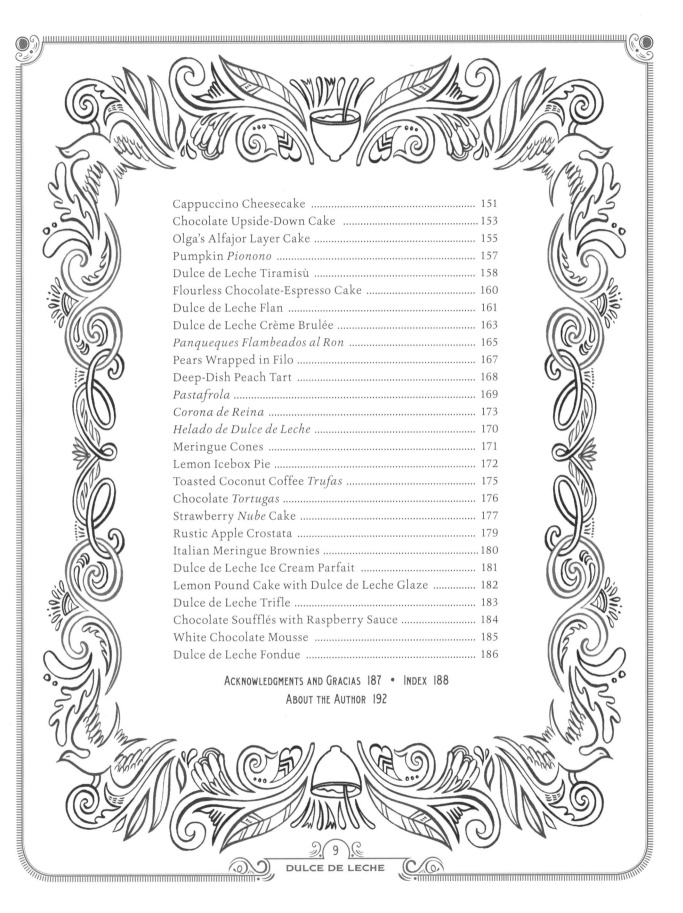

FOREWORD

The Special Ingredient

IAN KNAUER

THERE IS MAGIC INSIDE those jars that our mothers and grandmothers have filled and sealed. It is an ingredient that they give to us, and once we have it, there is no taking it away. If you are lucky enough to have had someone who has handed you such a jar, then you have that magic in you, too. It really doesn't matter what else was in the jar, or where she made it, or where in the world she was from.

My grandmother sweetened summer's ripest peaches with honey from my grandfather's hives and placed them in jars that seemed to glow with sunshine. Then she fed them to me. There is a moment, every summer, when I crack open my own jars of honey-sweetened peaches. I take a moment and breathe them in. I am reminded of the best parts of life and family and food. All of that from a jar of peaches.

Life has a way of getting away. Work is overwhelming. Family is chaotic. Love is confusing. And it's easy to forget, day to day, about the magic of life—the things and people and moments we want to remember. But it's in those jars. And if you were given that magic, it will be waiting for you when you're ready to open one.

Josephine's story of jars is all her own, yet it is familiar to me and to so many of us. Her Argentine grandmother stewed milk and sugar into a sticky, sweet milk jam and fed it to her family in jars and cakes and coffee. For her, those best parts of life come from a jar of dulce de leche. Imagine: a jar filled with caramelized milk and sugar—and magic.

This book will make you hungry, sure. And it will inspire you to cook. But there are lessons in these pages. There is patience, as Josephine and her husband, Gastón, had to learn how to sit quietly with the cooking milk. There is the intuition required to feel and know how to create the dulce de leche. There is practiced faith in its eventual outcome. Finally, there is the lesson of magic, and the recognition that this gift can and should be handed down to those we love.

IAN KNAUER

Host of *The Farm* on PBS, cookbook author and co-owner of
The Farm Cooking School in Stockton, New Jersey

INTRODUCCIÓN
The Sweet Soul Of Dulce De Leche

NO MATTER WHERE you come from or what language you speak, there will always be one food, more than any other, that you claim as your own. It is a part of your life, the flavor of comfort, and one taste of it represents home.

Without question, the humble boiled milk and sugar jam known as dulce de leche (duel-say day lay-chay) is just such a cultural phenomenon in Argentina. There, a bowlful of the creamy, gently sweet preserve sits on every breakfast table, and is stocked in every household's kitchen pantry. It is served in cafés in the morning, as well as for afternoon tea and all manner of desserts throughout the day. Commercial baby food is almost unheard of; instead, Argentine infants eat puréed fruits and vegetables sweetened with dulce de leche.

It even has earned a dedicated aisle in grocery stores, where every variety can be found—from the *tradicional* or *clásico*, the *del campo* (from the countryside), the *estilo colonial* or *criollo* (Spanish or Creole-style), the *con miel* (with honey) and the *para tortas y postres* or *repostero* (for cakes and desserts) to *chocolate*, and the *heladero*, used exclusively for making ice cream. And naturally, every region in Argentina claims to produce the best version.

Dulce de leche is so popular that on March 24, 2003, Argentina's Secretary of Culture issued a formal proclamation declaring dulce de leche part of the *Patrimonio Cultural Alimentario y Gastronómico Argentino*. This was Argentina's attempt to declare it a proprietary product, similar to France's rights over the Champagne valley, but I'm not sure that its neighbors–Uruguay, Chile, Paraguay and Brazil–would agree.

Dulce de leche's popularity also extends into Ecuador, Bolivia, Perú, Nicaragua, Costa Rica, Panamá, the Dominican Republic, Cuba, Puerto Rico and beyond. It is known as *doce de leite* in Brazil, *manjar blanco* in Perú, simply *manjar* in Chile, *arequipe* in Guatemala, Colombia and Venezuela, *fanguito* in Cuba and *cajeta* in México. The French preparation, *confiture de lait*, is very similar to the spreadable forms of dulce de leche.

Argentines actually claim the birthright to dulce de leche, as they link its beginnings to the nineteenth-century Argentine *caudillo* (political leader) Juan Manuel de Rosas. As the story goes, on a winter afternoon at the Rosas' house, their maid was making some *lechada*–a drink of milk and sugar that's boiled until it begins to caramelize–when she was distracted and left it unattended on the stove. By the time she returned, the *lechada* was burnt and had turned into a creamy golden-brown jam, which turned out to be a fortuitous and delectable mistake.

Over the centuries, traditional dulce de leche has never strayed from its modest beginning. Simplicity at its best, the classic recipe calls for slowly cooking fresh milk with sugar in a process similar to that of preserving fruits or making apple butter, except that raw milk does not require pectin to create a velvety texture. In the United States, the flavor, and indeed the dulce de leche itself, is often inaccurately described as mere "caramel" or relegated to an epicurean coffee-shop flavor. This is probably due to the FDA requirement that "milk caramel" appear on every label, because "milk jam" is somewhat ambiguous and not recognized in American food culture.

The truth is that dulce de leche has little in common with caramel, other than sharing that enticing golden color. In fact,

dulce de leche is a spreadable preserve that does not contain butter or cream and often has much less sugar than almost every commercial caramel lists on its label. In fact, it often has less sugar than most of the fruit jams and jellies Americans put in their shopping carts each week.

DULCE DE LECHE has been woven into the fabric of my life so completely that I cannot remember a time without it. My parents moved their young family of five children from Argentina to Pittsburgh when I was just one year old. My mother's parents, Dorita and Alfredo, were never far behind. They would visit us in America for six months at a time, usually every other year, and immediately after each visit, my siblings and I would count down the days until their next visit. Little did I know that Dorita's home cooking would become a major influence my adult life.

My grandparents always stayed in the apartment over our garage. Often, my mother had to referee the fights among us four girls as to whom got to sleep with Dorita. It never quite mattered who won; the losers would end up sneaking outside in flannel nightgowns and tiptoeing up the apartment staircase. Dorita would act surprised, but she and Alfredo were expecting us. Always a gentleman, my *abuelo*, who knew this meant another sleepless night on the floor for him, would have already pushed the twin beds together so all four girls and Dorita could fit across them. She sometimes allowed us to stay up late watching Johnny Carson on *la tele*. She would put curlers in our hair and polish our fingernails while heating up *leche con miel* or *con dulce de leche* before everyone finally went to sleep.

We always ate best when Dorita was in town. All of her food was from scratch—every meal, every day. She spent hours in the kitchen and was completely herself there. Wearing her apron and elbow-deep in flour, she would tell us secrets and family stories while we attempted to teach her English. Although she practiced, repeating words over and over in a thick accent, she never quite mastered the English language. Still, she never stopped trying.

On the other hand, Dorita did everything possible to bring Argentina to our home in Pittsburgh. She made sure that her grandchildren spoke Spanish fluently. She would make us recite a silly tongue twister over and over to get us in the habit of rolling our R's properly. "You may no longer live in Argentina," she would say, "but the Argentinean lives in you."

Dorita taught me everything I know in the kitchen, although she never allowed me to write down a recipe. Kneading dough, rolling out *ñoqui* (gnocchi) or *rosquitos* (shortbread doughnuts) and baking cakes and other desserts with her are some of my favorite memories. *"Un dedo de aceite, dos dedos de agua,"* she'd say. ("One finger of oil, two fingers of water.") From her, I learned that a good recipe never gets old, especially when you are working within your own legacy.

Bread, *medialunas* (crescent rolls), birthday cakes, flan, *piononos* (rolled cakes), *alfajores* (dulce de leche cookie sandwiches), *torta de nuez* (nut cake)—all these heavenly treats were part of Abuela Dorita's everyday repertoire, and she needed dulce de leche for almost every one of them. Since she couldn't find it in our supermarkets, she would stay up late into the night stirring a huge pot with gallons of milk to make sure we had fresh dulce de leche first thing in the morning for breakfast. And she always stashed her own personal reserves in the back of the cupboard for the next day's baking. This was simply part of her Argentine heritage, a part of her every day. From her, I inherited my passion for all things dulce de leche.

When Dorita left to go back home, so would the dulce de leche. My mother, love her, never had the time to make it from scratch, and, even if she did, it would have been gone by the next day. Mom would indulge us every once in a while by boiling several cans of condensed milk in a pressure cooker. It wasn't the real dulce de leche, but close enough to temporarily satisfy our cravings.

Second best to my grandparents' extended visits was our yearly trip to Argentina to visit them for the holidays. My birthday is just before Christmas, which meant that as a child I often celebrated my big day on the red-eye to Buenos Aires. However, it also meant that Dorita would be waiting for me with a special birthday cake— made with dulce de leche, of course. On my seventh birthday, she surprised me with a Barbie doll cake. The cake was the doll's large, ballroom-length skirt, coiffed with alternating ruffles made of dulce de leche and meringue. It was so beautiful I didn't want anyone to eat it.

During that same trip, my grandfather, Alfredo, showed me Argentina—his way. My parents and Dorita had left me with him for the weekend while they traveled south to the Patagonia with the rest of the family. When I awoke that Saturday morning, he said to me, "Jose, get dressed. Today I am going to show you my Argentina." Alfredo tucked a newspaper under his arm, took my hand and we walked several blocks to his home-away-from-home when Dorita was away—La Confitería Paris.

There it stood on the corner of 7th and 49th street in La Plata, the capital city of the province Gran Buenos Aires, its glass walls showcasing every variety of *pastelería* imaginable. As is typical in Argentine cafés, the place bustled all day long with locals who had come for a meal as well as those waiting in line to pick up their *facturas* (popular miniature pastries) for the afternoon *merienda*, or tea time.

In the café, generations of *Platenses* (people from La Plata) come together to discuss politics and the day's news, local writers and poets work at corner tables and men request windowside tables to watch the beautiful women passing by. That morning we shared the most delicious basket of fresh *medialunas*—some sweet, some savory, some simply stuffed with a dulce de leche center. My grandfather had several *cortaditos* (espresso "cut" with milk) while I sipped my *submarino* (a mug of piping-hot milk with a submerged chocolate bar). I can't tell you how long the two of us sat at that table, but that moment will stay with me for a lifetime.

I MOVED BACK TO ARGENTINA in my early twenties, and that's where I met Gastón. I knew almost immediately that I wasn't leaving Argentina—at least not without him. We married two years later. When he asked for my hand, I immediately said yes, on one condition: that we move to the United States for a couple of years, so that he could fully get to know me and understand that side of me. Back in Pittsburgh, we quickly found ourselves knee deep in our careers and the parents of four boys. Life was crazy, but I knew that no matter how busy I was, I had to feed my children with the same care and dedication that Dorita had shown me growing up. One thing was for sure: I would never let a family birthday slip by without making a special cake.

Before each birthday, I'd often find myself up late at night searching the Internet to track down the dulce de leche I needed for my cake. At that time, it was almost impossible to find it in my local stores, and when I did, it was usually past its prime and completely crystallized. As for boiling cans of condensed milk,

I had been put off years before when one can exploded on me, so that was not an option. I often just resorted to asking my mom and sister Corina, who lives in Miami, to bring dulce de leche in their suitcases; that worked, except for the times when Gastón, who enjoys nothing more than dulce de leche on toast with butter for breakfast, would find my hidden treasure before I had a chance to use it.

This went on for several years. And then, one morning I awoke with an innate determination to carry on my grandma's legacy of making dulce de leche, the *real* dulce de leche that she made for me as a child. Coffee in hand, I picked up the phone and called Dorita in Argentina. *"Abuela,"* I said with a sense of urgency, "I need your dulce de leche recipe."

She was still half asleep and trying to catch up with me. Reluctantly, impatiently, she began reciting the dulce de leche process by heart. She spoke in true Dorita fashion, without any detail as to measurements or cooking times: "First, boil the milk, then add the sugar, vanilla and a pinch of sodium bicarbonate. Continue to boil on medium-high heat, stirring continuously until it takes on a golden brown color and thicker consistency." *"Pero, abuela,"* I asked, "in what order do I add each ingredient?" I kept asking for details she was not able to give me, and she would say, *"Pero, Jose, ya te lo expliqué."* ("But, Josie, I already explained this.") Finally, after I had tired her out completely, she said, "When you commit yourself to the process and have a little faith in yourself, you'll get to know the feel of the milk, and it will turn out as planned."

I CAME HOME from work that day, and after tucking the kids into bed, began experimenting with Dori's dulce de leche "recipe"–if you could call it that. I went through several gallons of milk, but

I didn't care. I was committed to getting it right. It wouldn't turn out. Then it would. And then it began to turn out again, and again, and then even better. After several successes, and some failures, I learned how to sit quietly with the milk, and to tend to only the milk for the time it needed to transform into a golden spread.

Dorita turned ninety on September 25, 2009. More than a year had passed since I'd asked for her treasured recipe. By this time, Gastón and I were cooking up vast quantities of homemade dulce de leche for cakes, baby food, little sandwiches, cookies and, of course, the breakfast table. We sought out dairy farms where we could directly source the freshest raw milk possible and added our own touches, such as using vanilla beans instead of vanilla extract. To celebrate my grandmother's ninetieth birthday, friends and family—her two children, thirteen grandchildren, and fifteen great-grandchildren—all traveled to be with her in Argentina, and I decided that my gift to Dorita would be a jar of her dulce de leche.

I bottled an entire batch, put doilies on top of each jar and buried them in my suitcase. It was in that very same breakfast room where Dorita so often fed me as a child that she took the first bite of the dulce de leche I had made for her. Her eyes grew big. It had been years since she had made her own batch. As she spread it generously over her *tostada de pan integral* (whole wheat toast), she quietly said, *"Es tal cual como lo hacía yo. Gracias Jose."* ("It's just like I used to make it. Thank you Josie.") And with that one taste, we were both transported back thirty years, to when I was seven years old, enjoying Lincoln biscuits smothered with a fresh batch of her own dulce de leche. It was in that moment that I was reminded that something ordinary can become extraordinary, if we take the time to recognize it and appreciate it.

I last visited Dorita on her ninety-third birthday with a jar of dulce de leche under one arm and my daughter, who bears my mom's name, Poupée, in the other. Poupée was ten months old and meeting her great-grandmother for the first time. We ate a late lunch that day and topped it off with the post-meal *digestivo* (digestive drink), *licor de dulce de leche* in our coffees. Dorita peacefully passed away six months later. She was ready to go, and I knew I had to let her go. But she is still with me. I continue to celebrate Dorita in the everyday rituals of my family kitchen, especially when I find myself watching over a pot of boiling milk. It's there that I feel closest to Dorita. It's where we talk.

THIS COOKBOOK contains more than eighty recipes that show you how to incorporate dulce de leche into your own cooking repertoire so that you can enjoy it throughout the day: *en el desayuno* (at breakfast), *en la merienda* (at afternoon tea or coffee), *en la picada* (in small plates), *en la cena* (at dinner) and finally, at *la mesa de postre* (at the dessert table).

For me, there is nothing quite as satisfying as mastering the craft of artisanal dulce de leche and sharing the results with loved ones. The taste is pure ambrosia—far superior to most store-bought brands, with a light yet creamy texture. This natural slow food can become part of your legacy, too. Thus I begin with Dorita's traditional dulce de leche recipe, along with several variations that my family adores and that are called for throughout the book. If you choose not to make dulce de leche from scratch, make sure to buy the best commercial product you can find, with the shortest ingredient list.

Regardless of which dulce de leche you use, my sincerest wish is that you'll discover its magic. A couple of tablespoons enhances the flavor of grains, fruits, vegetables, cheeses, poultry and desserts, taking a dish from ordinary to outstanding with minimal effort and imbuing it with a mysterious goodness.

This is the good, simple food that I cook and eat again and again, and that has crept into my family traditions. Many of the recipes are passed down from my grandma Dorita. However, like me, others are neither exclusively from Argentina or America, but rather a cultural blending of ideas. I find that the best recipes always come with a story and remind me who I am, where I'm from and why a little dulce de leche can go a long way.

I'm grateful for the opportunity to preserve my family's traditions on these pages, along with the one ingredient that has informed my family life and continues to carry me forward. This is the belief that is always with me: Stay true to the food, stay true to family and tradition and continue to rediscover the flavors that leave a delicious stamp on our memories.

¡Buen provecho! Abuela Dorita, this one's for you.

Homemade is Best

IN THEORY, the time-honored craft of preserving dulce de leche is simple, yet few people seem to make their own anymore, mostly because it takes time and there are good quality products readily available in grocery and specialty stores. But as with most preserves, making your own dulce de leche results in a far superior ingredient that is less sweet and more flavorful than store-bought brands. Luckily, Dorita was still alive when I realized that I wanted to learn how to make dulce de leche, and she patiently shared her secrets with me.

Whether spread straight from the jar, baked into desserts, added to roasted vegetables, or simply formed into confections, dulce de leche is a pure and simple food that tastes and feels like magic, thanks to the Maillard reaction that promotes an irresistible caramelization. Just cow's milk, sugar and not a whole lot else goes into the golden spread that my abuela made so often throughout my childhood.

Despite the name, the type of milk used in dulce de leche is not universally the same: in México, it is made

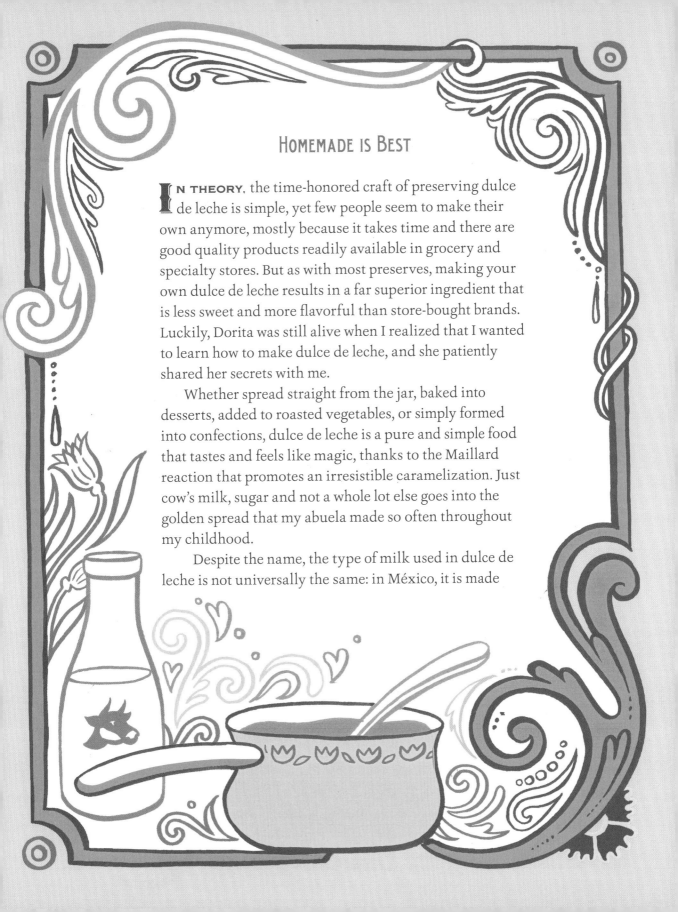

from goat's milk; in Cuba, from soured milk that's curdled and then sweetened, called *cortado*; and in the Dominican Republic, equal parts of milk and sugar are blended with cinnamon for a texture similar to fudge. Sometimes, in Puerto Rico, unsweetened coconut milk is preferred.

The French, too, have made this treat their own and ask for it by name— *confiture de lait*. Theirs is very similar to the spreadable forms of dulce de leche found in Argentina. In Haiti, it is known as *douce lait*. The Norwegian HaPå spread is a variation that is thicker and less sweet. Dulce de leche's reach can even be found as far east as Russia, where it is traditionally made by boiling cans of condensed milk in a water bath for several hours.

Take Your Sweet Time

ALL THAT IS REQUIRED to make a small batch of artisanal dulce de leche are four simple ingredients, a faithful stove, a heavy pot and time—a good two hours of it. I actually find the process to be quite meditative. The hum of boiling milk fills the air, along with its mesmerizing golden aroma, and before you know it, time slows and life seems a little simpler.

That said, milk is somewhat finicky and will scorch easily, so you cannot stray too far from the stove while it is cooking, especially toward the end. But I promise you this: making dulce de leche does not require any advanced expertise or kitchen artistry. With time and practice, the craft of making your own dulce de leche will become easier and easier—especially if you plan ahead.

Set aside a few hours of quiet kitchen time, place everything needed on the counter and make sure you have a podcast, a good book or some music to help you pass the time. Better yet, invite a few friends over to share the experience, and keep you company. (And taste the delectable results!) If you stick with it, you will understand that the skills my grandma Dorita passed down to me can become part of your legacy, too. Follow the recipes step-by-step, and there will be no surprises.

As with any dish, the quality of your ingredients makes all the difference. To create a superior dulce de leche, pay attention to the quality and freshness of the milk you use. All the recipes that follow call for raw or pasteurized cow's milk. If you can find raw cow's milk, rather than pasteurized, that's the best option. Yes, it is more expensive, and you may have to go to a farm to find it, but it's always worth the effort.

Raw milk that is bottled fresh, without heat, contains the essential fats and cream that make a better product. Gastón and I buy our raw milk from Le-Ara Farms in Worthington, Pennsylvania, one of only a few farms in our area licensed to sell raw milk directly to consumers. Fourth-generation farmers Lara Wilson Shields and her sister, Lesa, oversee a herd of more than sixty Holsteins and one Jersey cow, and they are committed to maintaining the farm's license for raw milk sales.

In the process of pasteurizing and homogenizing milk, a dairy takes out all of the fat from the milk that they will later use for cream and butter. The dairy then only adds a limited amount of cream back into the milk—1 percent, 2 percent or 3.2 percent for whole milk. It's the unprocessed cream in the raw milk that renders a creamier and more buoyant consistency to the

dulce de leche, as well as subtle nuances of flavor.

If possible, take note of the breed of cows that are providing the raw milk and their diet, as the flavor of the dulce de leche will be subtly impacted by both of these factors. The milk from Jersey cows, for example, has substantially more fat than milk from Holsteins. The consistency of dulce de leche made from raw milk will also slightly vary seasonally. For instance, in the winter farm-fresh milk has a higher fat content than in the summer, mainly due to the fact that cows eat more dry food than fresh grass then and are more confined.

Don't be concerned about the health risks of using raw milk in these recipes, as the milk will become pasteurized as it cooks. Pasteurized milk must be heated to 161 degrees for fifteen seconds. The dulce de leche, when done, will have boiled for more than an hour and a half at temperatures well above 200 degrees. If you are still concerned, if you cannot find the raw milk or if you simply prefer not to pay its higher price, whole pasteurized milk can always be used.

ALL MY DULCE DE LECHES

I HAVE INCLUDED five authentic dulce de leche recipes that each render a layered taste and melt-in-your-mouth texture. The traditional recipe, *dulce de leche clásico*, is the essential variety used throughout the day on its own or in sweet or savory meals. *Dulce de leche con miel* is preserved with raw honey instead of sugar. With its truly burnt sugar flavor, *dulce de leche criollo* has a dark, sophisticated quality. *Dulce de leche con chocolate* is for dark chocolate lovers everywhere, and the confectionary *dulce de leche repostero* is explicitly used in baked goods where a thicker consistency is required. All are far superior to the result you get from boiling a can of condensed milk in a pot of water. Each variation has its own distinctive character and nuanced complexity that is delicious on its own or for including in the recipes in this book. Of course, commercially produced dulce de leche will work in most of these recipes, too.

You will need a whole gallon of milk to yield 6 cups of the final spread;

using any smaller amount of milk simply isn't worth the two hours of your time. Once the dulce de leche is cool, I prefer to transfer it to clean mason jars with a good seal; it will keep in the refrigerator for up to one month.

If you plan to make dulce de leche to be used in a specific recipe, I suggest making it a day or two beforehand to allow enough time for it to cool to room temperature and to give yourself a break before continuing to make the whole dish. Please be sure to make the correct type of dulce de leche that is called for in the recipe, as each variety has a different texture and viscosity. Ultimately, as with any dish, the result will be affected by the type of dulce de leche you use. But you can rest assured it will be delicious.

TRADITIONAL DULCE DE LECHE

START TO FINISH COOKING TIME: 2 HOURS

I suggest that you begin by making this basic *dulce de leche clásico*, which is great for spreading on breads and crackers, mixing into hot cereal and coffee or adding to hot sauces. It lends itself to meals throughout the day, as it can be paired with savory and sweet dishes.

In fact, the only time it is not appropriate is for decorating baked goods or layering in cakes, as it is slightly too runny (see page 39 for instructions to thicken traditional dulce de leche). By mastering this traditional recipe, you'll get a good feel for the milk and can begin to explore new flavors or sugars to incorporate.

1 gallon pasteurized or raw whole cow's milk

1 teaspoon baking soda

4 cups granulated pure cane sugar

1 vanilla bean, split with seeds scraped into a small bowl

SPECIAL EQUIPMENT
12-quart heavy pot, preferably copper or aluminum, and a candy thermometer

Combine the milk and baking soda in a heavy 12-quart pot with a candy thermometer inserted and cook over medium high heat, stirring often with a wooden spoon or a flat wooden spatula, until the milk is warm, about 150°F. Gradually add the sugar, stirring constantly to keep the milk from sticking to the bottom and sides of the pot, until fully dissolved, about 5 minutes.

Put a heaping tablespoon of the milk mixture into a small bowl and stir in the vanilla seeds until dissolved, then stir the vanilla mixture into the pot, and continue to stir to keep the milk from sticking to the bottom and sides of the pot. As the milk begins to boil, it will foam and rise in the pot. If it appears that it will overflow, lower the heat as you continue to stir. Once the milk settles down, maintain a steady boil over medium-high heat and pay close attention, stirring every few minutes to keep the milk from sticking to the pot, for approximately 1 hour and 45 minutes more.

When the dulce de leche mixture coats the wooden spoon, is a deep golden color and reaches an approximate temperature of 215°F, test for doneness. Place a spoonful of dulce de leche on a cold plate, let it cool for a minute and tilt the plate. If it doesn't run, it is done. If it is still runny, continue to boil the mixture for five minutes more, then test again.

When the dulce de leche is done, remove the pot from the heat and immediately transfer the mixture to a metal bowl to keep it from sticking to the pot. Prepare an ice bath in an extra-large metal bowl. Place the bowl of dulce de leche into the ice bath, stirring the dulce de leche occasionally, for about 15 minutes to prevent overcooking or crystallizing. When the ice is melted, transfer the bowl of dulce de leche to a cooling rack and let cool for about 1 hour, or until it reaches room temperature.

If the cooled dulce de leche is lumpy or not as smooth as you would like, press the mixture through a fine-mesh sieve into another bowl. Spoon the dulce de leche into mason jars with a good seal or into any container with a tight-fitting lid and store in the refrigerator for up to a month.

The Wisdom of Dorita

JUST BEFORE HEADING BACK to Argentina one year, my grandparents wrote on our kitchen chalkboard: "Alfredo and Dorita wish our children and grandchildren much happiness during this Christmas season. *"¡No nos olviden!"* ("Don't forget us!") Dorita signed every letter with these three simple words. And that Christmas, she made sure she would be with us in spirit. During the days leading up to her departure, she and my mom, Poupée, stayed up into the wee hours of the morning making enough dulce de leche to last us through the holidays. I'd often hear them talking and laughing—my mom soaking in the last moments she would spend with her own mother until the next visit.

One night I awoke and came downstairs well past midnight, and as I approached the kitchen, I heard my mom, brother Olito and three sisters laughing. There was Dorita, barely five feet tall, standing atop our kitchen step stool, stirring a pot of boiling milk. My oldest sister, Verónica, who was probably fifteen at the time, was trying to lift her up while Dorita was fighting her off with a spoon. Verónica chuckled, "Let's see if I can pick up my *abuelita*!"

Half-asleep, I sank into my mom's lap. As the hours passed, we inhaled the sweet scent of the boiling milk and the *cariño* (love) that Dorita stirred into it. After tucking us all back into bed that night, Dorita and my mom jarred up the last batches. The dulce de leche tasted extra sweet that season. Mom would open a single jar each morning, and each of us made an effort to make it last a little longer. That was when I came to understand that dulce de leche is so much more than just food.

HONEY DULCE DE LECHE

START TO FINISH COOKING TIME: 1 HOUR, 40 MINUTES

This recipe for *dulce de leche con miel* celebrates small-batch honey—the raw stuff, harvested at peak season and bottled pure, without heat—and farm-fresh raw milk. The combination produces layers of flavor, some prominent on the nose, some developing as the dulce de leche hits the palate and others lingering in a long finish. Coarse-grained demerara sugar helps to round out the body of the dulce de leche, while the color and flavor will vary depending on where your honey is from and what flowers went into it.

As with all ingredients, the closer you can get to the actual source, the better off you'll be. I purchase my honey from our friend Joseph Zgurzynski, a second-generation beekeeper. Joe harvests his honey at Country Barn Farm located in my hometown, O'Hara Township, in July and again in September. The July harvest tends to be light in color with a pleasing floral aroma from basswood, honey locust, tulip poplar and blackberry flowers, and the dulce de leche from this early summer raw honey makes a delicious base for vinaigrette. The September harvest tends to be a very dark red with a surprisingly mild flavor provided by the red bamboo flowers growing along the rivers and streams near Pittsburgh. Its dulce de leche pairs exquisitely with freshly harvested Honeycrisp apples.

Due to the cost of the raw honey, this dulce de leche is more expensive to make than the others, but it's worth it. This is the one I spread on bread and crackers, roll up in *panqueques*, mix into my Greek yogurt and dip fruit into.

1 gallon pasteurized or raw whole cow's milk

1 teaspoon baking soda

1 (1 pound 1.5 ounce) box demerara sugar cubes

1½ cups raw honey

SPECIAL EQUIPMENT
12-quart heavy pot, preferably copper or aluminum, and a candy thermometer

Combine the milk and baking soda in a heavy 12-quart pot with a candy thermometer inserted and cook over medium high heat, stirring often with a wooden spoon or a flat wooden spatula, until the milk is warm, about 150°F. Add the sugar cubes, stirring constantly, until fully dissolved, for about 5 minutes. Add the honey, stirring constantly to keep the milk from sticking to the bottom and sides of the pot, until the milk boils.

As the milk begins to boil, it will foam and rise in the pot. If it appears that it will overflow, lower the heat as you continue to stir. Once the

CONTINUED

milk settles down, maintain a steady boil over medium-high heat and pay close attention, stirring every few minutes to keep the milk from sticking to the pot, for about 1 hour and 25 minutes more.

When the dulce de leche coats the wooden spoon, is a deep golden color and reaches an approximate temperature of 215°F, test it for doneness. Place a spoonful of dulce de leche on a cold plate, let it cool for a minute and tilt the plate. If it doesn't run, it is done. If it is still runny, continue to boil the mixture for five minutes more, then test again.

When the dulce de leche is done, immediately remove the pot from the heat and transfer the dulce de leche to a large metal bowl to keep it from sticking to the pot. Prepare an ice bath in an extra-large metal bowl. Place the bowl of dulce de leche in the ice bath, stirring the dulce de leche occasionally for about 15 minutes to prevent overcooking or crystallizing. When the ice is melted, transfer the bowl of dulce de leche to a cooling rack and let cool for about 1 hour, or until it reaches room temperature.

If the cooled dulce de leche is lumpy or not as smooth as you would like, press the mixture through a fine-mesh sieve into another bowl. Spoon into mason jars with a good seal or into any container with a tight-fitting lid and store in the refrigerator for up to a month.

BURNT CARAMEL DULCE DE LECHE

START TO FINISH COOKING TIME: 1 HOUR, 45 MINUTES

This amber *dulce de leche criollo* has a nutty burnt sugar flavor (almost like the top of a crème brulée) which is achieved by caramelizing some of the sugar before adding the milk; it is not to be missed. The recipe—a traditional favorite from Salta, the northwest province of Argentina with the largest production of sugarcane—is subtly sweeter than other dulce de leches. As a young boy, my husband, Gastón, lived in Salta and vividly remembers chewing on raw sugarcane his mother would cut from the side of the road. The deep, rich dark color and burnt amber flavor is the perfect complement to hot steel-cut oatmeal.

5⅓ cups granulated pure cane sugar, divided

1 gallon pasteurized or raw whole cow's milk

1 teaspoon baking soda

1 vanilla bean, split with seeds scraped into a small bowl

SPECIAL EQUIPMENT
12-quart heavy pot, preferably copper or aluminum, and a candy thermometer

Put ½ cup of the sugar in a heavy 12-quart pot with a candy thermometer inserted and cook over medium high heat, stirring constantly with a wooden spoon or a flat wooden spatula until the sugar caramelizes and turns a golden color, 5 to 7 minutes.

Carefully stir in the milk, which will bubble up and steam. When the milk reaches 150°F, gradually stir in the remaining sugar, the baking soda and vanilla seeds. (The milk will almost immediately turn a light beige color.) Continue to cook the mixture, stirring constantly to keep the milk from sticking to the bottom and sides of the pot, until the sugar is fully dissolved and the milk boils, 5 to 7 minutes. As the milk begins to boil, it will foam and rise in the pot. If it appears that it will overflow, lower the heat as you continue to stir. Once the milk settles down, maintain a steady boil over medium-high heat and pay close attention to the pot, stirring every few minutes to keep the milk from sticking to the pot, for approximately 1 hour and 45 minutes.

When the dulce de leche mixture coats the wooden spoon, is a deep golden color and reaches an approximate temperature of 215°F, test for doneness: Place a spoonful of dulce de leche on a cold plate, let it cool for a minute and tilt the plate. If it doesn't run, it is done. If it is still runny, continue to boil the mixture for five minutes more, then test again.

CONTINUED

When the dulce de leche is done, immediately remove the pot from the heat and transfer the dulce de leche to a metal bowl to keep it from sticking to the pot. Prepare an ice bath in an extra-large metal bowl. Place the bowl of dulce de leche into the ice bath, stirring the dulce de leche occasionally, for about 15 minutes to prevent overcooking or crystallizing. When the ice is melted, transfer the bowl of dulce de leche to a cooling rack and let cool for about 1 hour, or until it reaches room temperature.

If the cooled dulce de leche is lumpy or not as smooth as you would like, press the mixture through a fine-mesh sieve into another bowl. Spoon into mason jars with a good seal or into any container with a tight-fitting lid and store in the refrigerator for up to a month.

DARK CHOCOLATE DULCE DE LECHE

START TO FINISH COOKING TIME: 2 HOURS

Although adding chocolate to dulce de leche is quite a departure from the original recipe, the resulting flavor is genius. I have always considered *dulce de leche con chocolate* to be a tastebud doppelgänger for the Italian chocolate hazelnut spreads that are so popular. We spread it on just about anything, and as you'll see, I use it as a complementary ingredient in many recipes. Gastón first began making it by simply mixing natural cocoa into the traditional dulce de leche recipe near the end of the cooking process. For a quick dessert, I heat this in a fondue pot and pair it with angel food cake and seasonal fruits.

1 gallon pasteurized or raw whole cow's milk

1 teaspoon baking soda

4 cups granulated pure cane sugar

1 vanilla bean, split with seeds scraped into a small bowl

½ cup unsweetened cocoa powder

SPECIAL EQUIPMENT
12-quart heavy pot, preferably copper or aluminum, and a candy thermometer

Combine the milk and baking soda in a heavy 12-quart pot with a candy thermometer inserted and cook over medium high heat, stirring often with a wooden spoon or a flat wooden spatula, until the milk is warm, about 150°F. Gradually add the sugar, stirring constantly to keep the milk from sticking to the bottom and sides of the pot, until fully dissolved, about 5 minutes.

Put a heaping tablespoon of the milk mixture into a small bowl and stir in the vanilla seeds until dissolved, then stir the vanilla mixture into the pot, and continue to stir to keep the milk from sticking to the bottom and sides of the pot. As the milk begins to boil, it will foam and rise in the pot. If it appears that it will overflow, lower the heat as you continue to stir. Once the milk settles down, maintain a steady boil over medium-high heat and pay close attention, stirring every few minutes to keep the milk from sticking to the pot, for 1 hour and 20 minutes more.

Put 2 cups of the dulce de leche mixture into a small bowl and whisk in the unsweetened cocoa powder until incorporated, then stir the chocolate mixture back into the pot. Stir the dulce de leche almost constantly for about 20 more minutes more.

When the dulce de leche mixture coats the wooden spoon, is a deep brown color and reaches an approximate temperature of 215°F, test

CONTINUED

for doneness. Place a spoonful of dulce de leche on a cold plate, let it cool for a minute and tilt the plate. If it doesn't run, it is done. If it is still runny, continue to boil the mixture for five minutes more, then test again.

When the dulce de leche is done, remove the pot from the heat and immediately transfer the dulce de leche to a metal bowl to keep it from sticking to the pot. Prepare an ice bath in an extra-large metal bowl. Place the bowl of dulce de leche into the ice bath, stirring the dulce de leche occasionally, for about 15 minutes to prevent overcooking or crystallizing. When the ice is melted, transfer the bowl of dulce de leche to a cooling rack and let cool for about 1 hour, or until it reaches room temperature.

If the cooled dulce de leche is lumpy or not as smooth as you would like, press the mixture through a fine-mesh sieve into another bowl. Spoon into mason jars with a good seal or into any container with a tight-fitting lid and store in the refrigerator for up to a month.

CONFECTIONARY DULCE DE LECHE

START TO FINISH COOKING TIME: 1 HOUR, 50 MINUTES

Known in Argentina as *dulce de leche repostero*, this is the pièce de résistance, the one you will want to use when layering cakes, making ice cream or for general baking purposes. It has a much thicker consistency than traditional dulce de leche, so it holds its shape—it will never trickle down the side of a cake or spill out of a puff pastry. Corn syrup is used to round out the body of the dulce de leche and to give it that bakery-quality shine. Also, without the corn syrup, the agar-agar—a natural algae-based powder essential for thickening—produces an unpleasant gelatinous texture. Since confectionary dulce de leche is still not readily available in American grocery stores, there is an easy shortcut to thicken the traditional dulce de leche to the necessary consistency for baking (page 39).

1 gallon pasteurized or raw whole cow's milk

1 teaspoon baking soda

4½ cups plus 3 tablespoons granulated pure cane sugar, divided

1 cup high-fructose-free corn syrup

1 vanilla bean, split with seeds scraped into a small bowl

1½ teaspoons powdered agar-agar (not flakes)

SPECIAL EQUIPMENT

12-quart heavy pot, preferably copper or aluminum, and a candy thermometer

Combine the milk and baking soda in a heavy 12-quart pot with a candy thermometer inserted and cook over medium high heat, stirring often with a wooden spoon or a flat wooden spatula, until the milk is warm, about 150°F. Gradually add 4½ cups of the sugar, then add the corn syrup, stirring until fully dissolved.

Put a heaping tablespoon of the milk mixture into a small bowl and stir in the vanilla seeds until fully dissolved, then stir the vanilla mixture into the pot, stirring to keep the milk from sticking to the bottom and sides of the pot. As the milk begins to boil, it will foam and rise in the pot. If it appears that it will overflow, lower the heat as you continue to stir. Once the milk settles down, maintain a steady boil over medium-high heat and pay close attention, stirring every few minutes to keep the milk from sticking to the pot, for approximately 1 hour and 20 minutes.

Transfer a cup of dulce de leche mixture into a small bowl and whisk in the agar-agar and the remaining 3 tablespoons sugar, whisking until well combined and the sugar is dissolved. Stir the agar-agar mixture into the dulce de leche in the pot. The dulce de leche will have a darker golden color. Continue to boil, stirring constantly, for about 30 minutes.

CONTINUED

When the dulce de leche mixture is a deep golden color and reaches an approximate temperature of 215°F, test for doneness. Scrape the wooden spoon or spatula along the bottom of the pan. When it holds a mark and you can see the bottom of the pan, the dulce de leche is done.

Immediately remove the pot from the heat and transfer the dulce de leche to a metal bowl to keep it from sticking to the pot. Prepare an ice bath in an extra-large metal bowl. Place the bowl of dulce de leche into the ice bath, stirring the dulce de leche occasionally, for about 15 minutes to prevent overcooking or crystallizing. When the ice is melted, transfer the bowl of dulce de leche to a cooling rack and let cool for about 1 hour, or until it reaches room temperature.

If the cooled dulce de leche is lumpy or not as smooth as you would like, press the mixture through a fine-mesh sieve into another bowl. Spoon into mason jars with a good seal or into any container with a tight-fitting lid and store in the refrigerator for up to a month.

A Shortcut for Making Confectionary Dulce de Leche

Some of the recipes in this book call for a thickened form of confectionary *dulce de leche repostero* (page 37) for baking, since traditional dulce de leche is thinner and tends to drip when heated. When time is short, you can thicken both store-bought or your own homemade traditional dulce de leche with good results.

In a small bowl, whisk together 2 tablespoons of cornstarch and 1½ tablespoons whole milk until the cornstarch is fully dissolved. In the top of a double boiler, gradually bring 2 cups traditional dulce de leche to a slow boil, stirring occasionally, just until it begins to boil, then stir in the cornstarch mixture. Boil for about 5 minutes, stirring constantly, until the mixture begins to thicken. Immediately transfer the dulce de leche to a bowl and let it cool completely before using. It will continue to thicken as it cools. If the cooled dulce de leche is lumpy, press it through a fine-mesh sieve into another bowl.

BREAKFAST IN ARGENTINA tends to be a light meal, especially since dinners often run so late. A typical breakfast consists of strong black coffee or *café con leche*; *yerba mate* (my personal preference), a South American infusion made by steeping ground leaves and stems of the *yerba mate* plant; or *la leche* (milk) or *leche chocolatada* (hot chocolate milk) for children. This is accompanied with *tostadas*, thin slices of toast with butter, jam or dulce de leche; *facturas*, mini pastries; *medialunas*, half-moon crescent rolls; *tostados de jamón y queso*, toasted ham and cheese sandwiches pressed into paper-thin squares; *galletitas*, biscuit-like cookies or crackers and occasionally *fruta* (fruit). My mornings with Dorita always started with dulce de leche on toast or *galletitas Lincoln*.

While breakfast doesn't seem to be much of a big deal, it is always delicious. The coffee is usually fresh roasted espresso, no matter the café or restaurant, and the pastries are spectacular. *Panaderías* (neighborhood bakeries) sell out of most of their fresh bread and *facturas* by noon and fill the streets with the incredible smell of fresh-baked loaves and *medialunas*.

In any case, the breakfast table is not complete without a tub of dulce de leche.

DARK CHOCOLATE BANANA BREAD

This is the quickest and easiest of sweet bread recipes and very satisfying. While most banana breads tend to be on the sweeter side, the addition of dark cocoa powder strikes a nice balance with the banana and dulce de leche. To achieve the best flavor, use very ripe, plump bananas. If you have ugly bananas that are on the verge of spoiling but are unable to make this bread right away, peel and freeze them until ready to use.

2 cups all-purpose flour

¾ cup granulated sugar

¼ cup dark cocoa powder

1½ teaspoon baking powder

1 teaspoon salt

½ cup (1 stick) unsalted butter, softened

⅔ cup traditional dulce de leche

2 large eggs

1 tablespoon vanilla extract

3 very ripe bananas, mashed

Preheat the oven to 350°F. Butter and flour a 9-by-5-inch loaf pan. Sift together the flour, sugar, cocoa powder, baking powder and salt in a large bowl. In a separate bowl, with a handheld mixer on medium speed, cream the butter with the dulce de leche until light and fluffy, then beat in the eggs, vanilla and bananas until well combined. Stir in the flour mixture until just combined.

Pour the batter into the loaf pan and bake 50 to 60 minutes until a toothpick inserted into the center of the bread comes out almost clean. Cool for at least 15 minutes in the pan, then turn the cake out onto a wire cooling rack. Cut into thick slices to serve.

TORTA DE NUEZ

This was Grandma Dorita's nut cake—her classic. It made an appearance at every birthday, holiday and Sunday *asado,* and we always ate leftovers the next morning for breakfast. *"¿Quien quiere ser mi Juanita?"* Dorita would ask as she reached for her apron. ("Who wants to be my Juanita?") Juanita, little Jane, was the kitchen assistant of a well-known Argentine TV cook, Doña Petrona, who was Argentina's own Julia Child. Juanita became an icon herself, and it's very common in Argentina when someone is cooking and needs help to refer to the person helping them as Juanita. I was often lucky enough to be Dorita's Juanita, and would perch myself on a stool next to her, cracking the eggs and pounding the walnuts.

Dorita always served this cake with dulce de leche on the side.

5 large eggs, separated

Pinch of salt

2 cups walnuts

½ cup (1 stick) unsalted butter, chilled and cut into cubes

2 cups granulated sugar

1 cup whole milk

5 cups all-purpose flour

Traditional dulce de leche or dark chocolate dulce de leche, for serving

Preheat the oven to 350°F. Butter and flour a 10-inch tube cake pan. Put the egg whites and a pinch of salt in the bowl of a stand mixer fitted with the whisk attachment and whisk on high speed until slightly stiff peaks form. Set aside.

In a food processor, pulse the walnuts until crushed to a soft, crumb-like consistency.

Put the butter in a clean bowl of the stand mixer fitted with the paddle attachment and beat on high speed until light and fluffy, then slowly add the sugar, beating until well combined. Add the egg yolks, one at a time, beating each until combined before adding the next. Reduce the speed to low, then add the milk and beat until incorporated. Slowly add the flour, mixing until incorporated. Mix in the reserved crushed walnuts. With a spatula, carefully fold in the reserved egg whites.

Carefully transfer the batter to the cake pan and bake 40 to 45 minutes or until a toothpick inserted into the center of the cake comes out clean. Cool for 30 minutes in the pan, then turn the cake out onto a wire cooling rack to cool completely.

Serve slices of the cake with a dollop of dulce de leche. The cake keeps, tightly wrapped in plastic wrap, at room temperature for 3 days, or in the refrigerator for up to 1 week.

BLUEBERRY COFFEE CAKE

Buttermilk always ensures a moist cake, but the combination of fresh blueberries, dulce de leche and a sweet crumble topping takes it over the top. Whenever I have company and blueberries are in season, I double the recipe (see Variation, below).

FOR THE BATTER

½ cup granulated sugar

1½ cups all-purpose flour

½ teaspoon baking powder

½ teaspoon baking soda

4 tablespoons unsalted butter, chilled and cut into small cubes

1 large egg, beaten

½ cup buttermilk

½ teaspoon vanilla

FOR THE FILLING

½ cup traditional dulce de leche

½ cup blueberries

FOR THE TOPPING

¼ cup granulated sugar

¼ cup all-purpose flour

2 tablespoons unsalted butter, chilled and cut into small cubes

MAKE THE BATTER: Preheat the oven to 350°F. Lightly grease an 8-inch round or square baking pan with nonstick cooking spray. In a mixing bowl, stir together the sugar, flour, baking powder and baking soda. With a pastry cutter, cut in the butter until the mixture resembles fine crumbs. In another bowl, combine the egg, buttermilk and vanilla and add to the flour mixture, stirring just until moistened. Scrape half of the batter into the baking pan and spread evenly.

ADD THE FILLING AND REMAINING BATTER: Spread the dulce de leche over the batter and scatter the blueberries evenly on top. Drop the remaining batter in small mounds on top of the filling.

MAKE THE CRUMBLE TOPPING: In a small bowl, combine the sugar and flour and cut in the butter with the pastry cutter until the mixture resembles fine crumbs. Sprinkle the topping evenly over the batter.

Bake for 40 to 45 minutes or until the cake is golden brown. Cool for 20 minutes in the pan, then turn the cake out onto a wire cooling rack to cool slightly. Serve warm.

VARIATION: To serve a crowd, double the recipe and bake the coffee cake in a 13-by-9-by-2-inch pan for 45 to 50 minutes.

APPLE MUFFINS

At our house, weekday mornings tend to get a bit harried. To make sure that the children have something good to eat for breakfast, I bake these sweet, crunchy-topped muffins on Sunday, pack them in a large resealable plastic bag and tuck them away in the pantry. As the kids run for the bus, I have this portable power breakfast, loaded with fresh apples, at the ready.

½ cup (1 stick) unsalted butter, softened

¾ cup confectionary dulce de leche

½ cup brown sugar, divided

1 large egg

¼ cup sour cream

1 cup whole wheat flour

1 cup all-purpose flour

1 teaspoon baking powder

1 teaspoon baking soda

1 teaspoon ground cinnamon

¼ teaspoon salt

2 cups peeled, cored and chopped apples (about 1½ large apples)

Preheat the oven to 375°F. Butter and flour a 1-cup muffin pan or line pan with paper baking cups. In a mixing bowl, beat the butter, confectionary dulce de leche and ¼ cup brown sugar on medium speed with an electric mixer until fluffy. Add the egg and mix well, stopping once to scrape down the sides and bottom of the bowl. Reduce the speed to low, then gently mix in the sour cream.

In a separate bowl, stir together the whole wheat flour, all-purpose flour, baking powder, baking soda, ground cinnamon and salt until combined. Slowly add the flour mixture to the batter, beating on low speed until just combined. Fold in the apples.

Using an ice cream scoop, divide the batter evenly among the muffin cups and sprinkle the remaining ¼ cup brown sugar on top. Bake for 25 to 30 minutes or until the muffins are golden brown and a toothpick inserted into the center comes out clean. Cool for 5 minutes in the pan, then turn the muffins out onto a wire cooling rack to cool completely. The muffins are incredibly moist and keep in a sealed plastic bag at room temperature for up to 1 week.

PANQUEQUES
con Dulce de Leche

Panqueques are one of Gastón's specialties. Should you ask him to share his recipe, he's quick to answer, "It's easy. Three-two-one: three eggs, two cups of milk and one cup of flour." Like my Grandma Dorita's, Gastón's recipes are often vague. Fortunately, I was brought up in a kitchen with ambiguous directions and inexact measurements—*puñados, dedos, pizcas y poquitos* (handfuls, fingers, pinches and little bits). These *panqueques* are to the Argentine what *crêpes* are to the French, but slightly thicker, lighter and fluffier. *Panqueques* are easy to make and fun to serve; just remember that you'll need to wait a few hours for the batter to chill.

3 large eggs

2 cups milk

1 cup all-purpose flour, preferably unbleached

4 tablespoons butter, melted, plus more for coating the pan

2 tablespoons granulated sugar

¼ teaspoon salt

Traditional or dark chocolate dulce de leche, for serving

Put the eggs, milk, flour, melted butter, sugar and salt in a blender and blend for 30 seconds or until smooth. Scrape down the mixture from the sides of the blender and repeat if necessary. Cover and chill for at least 1 hour (2 hours is preferable) and up to 24 hours.

If the chilled batter has separated, gently stir it until it comes back together. Lightly butter a 6- or 7-inch nonstick pan and heat over medium-high heat until hot. Lift the pan from the heat and pour in 2 to 3 tablespoons of batter, tilting and rotating the pan to coat the surface. Return the pan to the heat and cook the *panqueque* until almost dry on top and lightly browned on the edges, about 1 minute. Loosen the edges with a spatula and, using your fingers or a spatula, flip over the *panqueque* and cook the other side for about 15 seconds, or until lightly browned. Make more *panqueques* with the remaining batter in the same manner, wiping the pan with butter (we peel back the paper on the stick of butter and wipe it on the pan), as needed, and stacking the *panqueques* after they are cooked.

TO SERVE: Spread the top of each *panqueque* with about 2 teaspoons of dulce de leche and fold or shape as desired (see Sidebar below).

The unfilled stack of *panqueques* keeps, wrapped in plastic wrap, in the refrigerator for up to 3 days. Spread with dulce de leche just before serving.

How Do You Take Your Panqueque?

After spreading with dulce de leche, *panqueques* may be shaped in a variety of ways depending on one's own personal preference. We choose between the cigarette, which is filled and rolled like a cylinder, or the quarter-moon, folded with panache and made by spreading the filling on half of the *panqueque* and folding it over once then again. For breakfast, Gastón serves *panqueques* with dulce de leche and jam; for lunch, he fills them with soft cheese and dulce de leche; and for a special dessert he stuffs them with dulce de leche then flambés them with rum and caramelized sugar.

WAFFLES BELGAS DE DULCE DE LECHE

These Belgian waffles take me back to my childhood and to the picturesque *casas de té* (tea houses) that are typical in the Patagonia, the southernmost region of Argentina. The tea rooms—many run by descendants of the original settlers—are housed in immaculately kept cottages reminiscent of Swiss villages. Just a couple of years ago, my boys and I were lured into our neighborhood Williams-Sonoma by the aroma of Belgian waffles. Shortly thereafter, my son Lucas asked *Papá Noel* for a waffle maker, and we've been experimenting with recipes ever since. One morning, we discovered that we were out of sugar, so we replaced it with dulce de leche and created these wonderfully full-bodied egg white waffles with just a hint of sweetness and an extra-light, melt-in-your-mouth texture. I'm often asked if they are made with whole wheat flour, as the dulce de leche imparts a golden-brown color.

2 cups all-purpose flour

2 teaspoons baking powder

½ teaspoon salt

4 large eggs, separated

1 cup traditional dulce de leche, plus more for serving

4 tablespoons unsalted butter, melted

1 cup whole milk

Confectioners' sugar, for garnish

SPECIAL EQUIPMENT

Belgian waffle maker

Preheat the waffle iron.

In a medium bowl, mix together the flour, baking powder and salt. Set aside.

In a large bowl, whisk together the egg yolks and dulce de leche until fully incorporated, then whisk in the melted butter and milk, whisking until combined. Slowly whisk in the flour mixture, whisking just until blended and smooth. Do not overmix.

Put the egg whites in the bowl of a stand mixer fitted with the whisk attachment and beat on high speed until soft peaks form, about 1 minute. Using a rubber spatula, gently fold the egg whites into the waffle batter just until incorporated. Do not overmix.

Coat the waffle iron with nonstick cooking spray and pour enough batter in the iron to just cover the waffle grid. Close the iron and cook each waffle until golden brown, about 4 to 5 minutes. Transfer the waffles to individual plates and dust with confectioner's sugar. Serve immediately with dulce de leche.

CHALLAH FRENCH TOAST

I'm a firm believer that the best French toast is made with dense, high-quality bread—such as challah or brioche loaf—that leaves you with a creamy interior and crunchy exterior. The slices should be neither too thin nor too thick: if it's thinly sliced, the bread will be too flimsy when dipped in the custard; if the slices are too thick, they'll never cook into the center. The ideal thickness is ¾ to 1 inch. I prefer my French toast on the thicker side, so that it can soak up extra custard and, quite frankly, keep me from going back for seconds. If you've never had French toast with dulce de leche, you are in for a treat.

3 cups whole milk or almond milk

½ cup traditional dulce de leche

3 teaspoons vanilla extract

¼ teaspoon salt

6 large eggs

8 (1-inch-thick) slices challah bread, or bread of your choice

2 tablespoons unsalted butter

Traditional dulce de leche, for serving

In a large shallow bowl, whisk together the milk, dulce de leche, vanilla and salt until combined, then whisk in the eggs until well combined. Soak several slices of the challah in the egg mixture, turning them over once, until just soaked through.

Melt the butter in a large skillet over medium heat and add as many pieces of challah as will fit comfortably. Cook the bread, adjusting the heat as necessary so the bread will cook halfway through without burning, for 3 to 4 minutes or until the underside is golden brown.

Flip over the bread with a spatula, reduce the heat to medium-low, and cook 3 to 5 minutes more or until the underside is golden brown and the bread is just cooked through. Transfer the French toast to a platter and serve with gently warmed dulce de leche.

MEDIALUNAS RELLENAS

(Sweet Crescent Rolls Filled with Dulce de Leche)

The *medialuna* (half-moon) is Argentina's signature crescent roll and can be found in any café throughout the country. It's enjoyed first thing in the morning, often with a *café con leche*, and makes an appearance again around 5 p.m. at *la merienda*. There are several different types—the most common, *la medialuna común* or *de manteca*, is made with butter; it is very fluffy, smaller than a typical croissant and sweeter, as it is lightly glazed with sugar syrup right out of the oven. The *medialuna de grasa* is made with lard; it is much slimmer and has a more savory taste and flaky texture. Then there's the *medialuna rellena*, typically a sweet version filled with dulce de leche, *dulce de membrillo* (quince paste) or *crema pastelera* (custard).

Making *medialunas* from scratch is not difficult, but you'll need to set aside several hours, as the dough must chill in stages. I bake these for special occasions and often prepare the pastry dough the day before. They are absolutely wonderful, but when time is short, see the Variation on page 52.

2 cups whole milk

1 cup granulated sugar

1¾ ounces fresh yeast, or ½ ounce active dry yeast

1 teaspoon salt

3 large eggs, at room temperature, divided

6½ cups unbleached bread flour

2 cups (4 sticks) cold unsalted butter

1¼ cups confectionary dulce de leche

FOR THE GLAZE

¼ cup raw honey

SPECIAL EQUIPMENT

An instant-read thermometer

Warm the milk in a small saucepan over low heat until it reaches 110°F on an instant-read thermometer, and transfer it to the bowl of a stand mixer fitted with a dough hook. Add 1 tablespoon of the sugar and the yeast and stir to dissolve. Let stand until the yeast fully dissolves and the mixture becomes bubbly, about 5 minutes.

With the mixer on low speed, slowly add the ingredients, one at a time, incorporating each before adding the next: the salt, the remaining sugar, 2 eggs and the flour. Continue to knead with the dough hook until the dough comes together, about 3 minutes. Transfer to a lightly floured surface and continue to knead by hand just until a smooth dough is formed, 2 to 3 more minutes. Form the dough into a round and transfer to a large bowl. Let the dough rise in the refrigerator, covered with plastic wrap, for 30 minutes.

Meanwhile, on a work surface, place the cold sticks of butter side by side between two pieces of plastic wrap and pound with a rolling pin to form a fairly uniform square block of butter, about ¼ inch thick. Refrigerate, wrapped in the plastic wrap, for about 10 minutes.

Transfer the chilled dough to a lightly floured surface and roll it into a rectangle, about ½ inch thick.

Unwrap the chilled block of butter and place it in the center of the rectangle of dough, leaving a border of dough around it. Fold the edges of the dough over the butter like a package to form a square, then fold the square in half to make a rectangle. Finally, fold the rectangle in half to make a small square. Wrap the dough in plastic wrap and refrigerate for 1 hour.

Transfer the chilled dough to a lightly floured work surface. Carefully roll out the dough into a rectangle, about ½ inch thick. If the butter breaks through the dough, fold some dough over it to reseal. Then, as above, fold the edges of dough to form a square, then fold the square in half to make a rectangle. Finally, fold the rectangle in half to make a small square. Wrap the dough in plastic wrap and refrigerate for 1 more hour.

Repeat the rolling and folding and chilling process two more times. (The dough needs a total of 4 turns, with 1 hour of chilling between turns.) After the fourth turn, the dough can be used immediately or wrapped in plastic wrap and stored in the refrigerator for up to 1 day.

When you are ready to form and bake the *medialunas*, preheat the oven to 375°F. Lightly coat one large baking sheet (or two medium baking sheets) with nonstick cooking spray. Transfer the dough to a lightly floured work surface and cut the small square of dough in half. Return one of the halves to the refrigerator to keep cold.

Roll out the remaining half into a rectangle about ½ inch thick. With a sharp knife, cut off the edges to form a uniform rectangle, then cut the rectangle horizontally in half to form 2 rectangular strips. Cut 8 congruent equilateral triangles across the strips. Pull apart the triangles and set aside.

Working with one triangle at a time, gently stretch the corners to form a larger triangle. Add a teaspoon of dulce de leche towards the middle of the larger end of the triangle. Starting from the widest end, roll the dough over the dollop of dulce de leche and pinch the dough around it to make sure it doesn't seep out while baking. Continue rolling from the base to the tip, stretching the dough slightly as you go, until the tip is under the roll. Pull the two ends of the roll

CONTINUED

together, pinching each to form a crescent shape. Place on the baking sheet.

Form more *medialunas* in the same manner and place on the baking sheet, touching the one in front and covering the tips to prevent them from burning. Roll out the remaining chilled dough in the same manner and form more *medialunas*, transferring them to the baking sheet. Let the *medialunas* rise for 40 minutes.

After they have risen, beat 1 egg with 1 tablespoon of water. Brush the *medialunas* with the egg wash and bake for 20 minutes or until puffed and golden. Remove from the oven and let cool slightly on the baking sheet.

MAKE THE SUGAR GLAZE: Gently heat the honey and ½ cup water in a small saucepan over low heat, stirring with a wooden spoon, until the honey has completely dissolved. Increase the heat and bring to a boil, then simmer, without stirring, for about 3 minutes or until the mixture has thickened slightly.

While the *medialunas* are still hot, brush the tops with the glaze. They will continue to absorb the glaze as they cool on the baking sheet.

VARIATION: When time is tight, you can use refrigerated crescent rolls instead of making your own. Separate the rolls into triangles. Working with one triangle at a time, add a spoonful of dulce de leche towards the middle of the longest side. Starting there, roll the dough over the dulce de leche and pinch the dough around it to make sure it won't seep out while baking. Continue to roll the stuffed dough triangle to its tip, then pinch the edges to form a crescent shape. Transfer it to a baking sheet coated with nonstick cooking spray. Make more rolls in same manner. Lightly beat 1 egg with 1 tablespoon of water to make an egg wash and brush evenly over the rolls. Bake the rolls according to the package directions. After removing the *medialunas* from the oven, brush tops with the sugar glaze.

DULCE DE LECHE TWISTY ROLLS

I've made this bread with my oldest son, Lucas, so many times, he knows it by heart. Baking teaches children many things, such as measuring, following directions, working with their hands and, most importantly, patience—especially when dealing with dough that rises not once, but twice. (You'll need to set aside 2 hours total to make these.) Be sure to bake the rolls on a rimmed baking sheet, as the dulce de leche is likely to bubble over. And don't forget to serve these treats with a glass of warm milk or cup of tea, as they have the ideal consistency for dunking.

FOR THE DOUGH

1 ounce fresh yeast or ¾ ounce active dried yeast (three ¼-ounce packages)

2 generous tablespoons of raw honey

6 to 8 cups unbleached bread flour

2 tablespoons sea salt

FOR THE FILLING

1 cup (2 sticks) unsalted butter, softened

1 cup traditional dulce de leche

MAKE THE DOUGH: In a bowl, dissolve the yeast and raw honey in 1 cup of tepid water and let stand until the yeast dissolves and the mixture becomes bubbly, about 5 minutes.

Put 6 cups of the flour and salt in a large bowl or on a clean surface and make a well in the center. Pour the yeast mixture into the well and with one hand make circular movements to slowly mix in more and more of the flour until all the yeasty liquid is soaked up. Then slowly pour another cup of tepid water into the center and gradually incorporate as much of the remaining flour as necessary to make a moist dough, adding more tepid water, a couple of drops at a time, as needed. Knead the dough with your hands for 5 minutes. If the dough begins to stick to your hands, pat them in flour and rub them together.

When the dough is a smooth consistency, flour both hands and lightly flour the top of the dough. Form the dough into a roundish shape and place it on a baking sheet. Score the top of the dough deeply with a knife and let it rise in a warm place, free from drafts, for about 40 minutes.

Once the dough has doubled in size, punch it down and knead for a minute or so. Divide the dough into 2 equal parts. Form the dough into rounds and transfer each to a baking sheet. Let rise a second time, about 40 minutes or until doubled in size. At this point, the dough can be baked immediately or wrapped in plastic wrap and kept in the refrigerator for up to 1 day.

CONTINUED

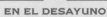

After the second rising, transfer each piece of dough to a floured surface and form each into a square shape. Working with one square at a time, roll the dough out about 7 inches wide, then roll the other way to achieve a long rectangle, about ¼ inch thick. Roll out the remaining dough in the same manner. The rectangles should be roughly uniform in width and thickness so the rolls will bake evenly.

MAKE THE FILLING AND BAKE THE ROLLS: Preheat the oven to 400°F. Lightly coat a large rimmed baking sheet with sides with butter or cooking spray. In a bowl, mix together the butter and dulce de leche until fully incorporated and creamy.

Using a spatula, spread half of the dulce de leche mixture evenly and thinly on the top of each rectangle. Starting with the long side of the dough, roll up the rectangles, jelly-roll fashion, and cut into 1-inch-wide slices. Place the slices, cut side up, about ½ inch apart on the baking sheet and bake about 20 minutes until golden. Cool for 20 minutes on the baking sheet, then remove the rolls while they are still warm. Serve warm or transfer to a wire cooling rack to cool.

VARIATIONS: For chocolate lovers, sprinkle the dulce de leche filling with 6 ounces chopped or grated dark chocolate before rolling up the dough; for those who like savory and sweet, layer 8 to 10 slices of prosciutto on top of the dulce de leche before pulling the dough over the filling.

Holiday Breakfast Wreaths

I make Christmas morning a bit more festive with this indulgent breakfast treat. I use the Dulce de Leche Twisty Rolls recipe on page 53, but instead of making rolls, I shape each dough round into the form of a wreath. To make the wreaths extra delicious, I add dark chocolate or prosciutto.

Once you have rolled the first dough into a jelly roll, press the edge to seal and place, seam side down, on a parchment paper–lined baking sheet. Shape it into a ring, pressing the ends together. Cut the ring on a bias at 2-inch intervals, from the outer edge towards the middle of the ring, leaving a half inch or so from the middle of the ring. Gently pull and twist the cut pieces to show the filling. Cover the dough and let it rise in a warm place, free from drafts, for 1 hour or until doubled in bulk. Form the second roll in the same manner.

Melt 4 tablespoons of butter and brush it over the wreaths. Bake in a preheated 350°F oven for 30 to 40 minutes or until golden. Cool on the baking sheet for 10 minutes, then transfer to a wire cooling rack.

APPLE-CINNAMON OATMEAL

We live in Pittsburgh, which means that at least eight months out of the year, the mornings are pretty cold. This is my go-to breakfast during the chilly months of the school year. It only takes minutes to make, and I know it will get my kids through the first couple of hours of school until lunchtime. I prefer to use almond milk for its nutty flavor and lighter consistency. A sprinkle of slivered raw almonds on top adds more flavor and crunch.

1 apple, peeled and finely chopped

½ tablespoon unsalted butter

¾ teaspoon ground cinnamon

3½ cups unsweetened almond milk

¼ cup traditional dulce de leche

2¾ cups old-fashioned oats

Slivered raw almonds, for serving

In a saucepan, combine the apple, butter, cinnamon and ½ cup water. Cook over medium heat, stirring frequently and adding more water as necessary to maintain a moist consistency, until the apples are soft, about 5 minutes. Stir in the almond milk and bring to a boil. Lower the heat, then add the dulce de leche and oats and continue to cook, stirring frequently, for 5 minutes or until the oatmeal thickens. Serve immediately, topped with the almonds.

VARIATION

BAKED APPLE-CINNAMON OATMEAL WITH ALMONDS

The beauty of a baked oatmeal casserole is that it can be prepared the night before, refrigerated, then baked off the next morning. The night before, double the ingredients for the Apple-Cinnamon Oatmeal with Almonds (recipe above) and make the recipe. When you remove the oatmeal from the stove, let it cool for 10 minutes. Lightly coat a 13-by-9-inch glass or ceramic baking dish with nonstick cooking spray and pour in the oatmeal mixture. Cover with foil and refrigerate overnight.

The next morning, bake the covered casserole in a 350°F oven for 20 minutes. Remove the foil and bake for another 20 to 25 minutes or until the top is nicely golden and the oatmeal mixture is set. Let the casserole cool for 5 to 10 minutes, then cut into large square pieces. Serve with a light drizzle of gently warmed honey or maple syrup.

PEPITA GRANOLA

While *pepitas*, a Spanish culinary term for pumpkin seeds, are a very popular snack in most Latin American countries, in Argentina you will have better luck finding them in the bakery section of a local supermarket. Argentine *pepitas* are essentially bite-sized butter cookies topped with a dollop of *dulce de membrillo* (quince jam). Here in the United States, you will commonly find raw, unhulled green pumpkin seeds in any store that carries bulk or organic products. *Pepitas* can be eaten whole (no need to worry about the outer shell) and are delicious alone or roasted with olive oil and salt.

My children enjoy making sundaes with bowls of Greek yogurt, so I set out this granola and the freshest seasonal fruits and berries I can find and let them go to town.

2 cups old-fashioned rolled oats

1 cup raw pepitas (green pumpkin seeds)

1 cup raw sliced almonds

⅔ cup light brown sugar

1 cup confectionary or traditional dulce de leche

2 teaspoons salt

¼ teaspoon cayenne pepper

4 tablespoons canola oil

Preheat the oven to 325°F. Line a rimmed baking sheet with parchment paper and lightly grease the paper with nonstick cooking spray. In a large bowl, mix together the oats, pepitas, almonds, brown sugar, dulce de leche, salt, cayenne pepper and oil until well combined. Transfer the granola mixture to the baking sheet and spread it out, flattening it evenly with slightly wet hands.

Bake the granola for 25 to 30 minutes or until golden brown and crispy. Turn off the oven, prop open the door, and let the granola sit in the oven for 10 minutes more. Transfer the baking sheet to a rack to cool completely. Break the granola into pieces and transfer to an airtight container. The granola keeps refrigerated, for up to 2 weeks.

CANDIED BACON
WITH SOFT~BOILED EGGS

The secret to preparing these candied *soldados*, or soldiers, so that they are crisp rather than chewy is to slow-roast the bacon in a low oven for up to an hour. Be patient; the result is worth the wait! At our house we ration out the bacon equally to each family member before digging into the eggs to avoid any arguments. Keep this dish in mind as a starter, snack or even for lunch alongside mixed salad greens. On their own, the candied-bacon *soldados* make a great hors d'oeuvre.

½ cup traditional dulce de leche

½ teaspoon cayenne pepper

1 pound center cut, uncured thick-sliced bacon, or your favorite high-quality bacon, sliced

2 sprigs fresh rosemary

6 large eggs

Salt and freshly ground pepper

Preheat the oven to 325°F. Line a rimmed baking sheet with aluminum foil and fit with a wire rack. Put the dulce de leche and cayenne pepper in a bowl and mix well. Add the bacon and toss gently with your hands until evenly coated. Place the bacon in a single layer on the wire rack and put sprigs of rosemary on top. Refrigerate for 10 minutes to set.

Bake the bacon until slightly dark (not burnt) and crispy, about 45 to 55 minutes total, rotating the pan halfway through baking and removing the end pieces and the rosemary after about 40 minutes if they are browning quickly. Let cool for 15 minutes.

While the bacon is cooling, bring a small pan of salted water to a boil. Carefully lower the eggs into the boiling water with a slotted spoon and boil for 5 minutes. Drain the eggs, cut off the lids and serve with a pinch of salt and pepper in egg cups for individual servings or in an egg carton if serving family style. Serve the bacon soldiers alongside for dipping into the eggs.

PANCETTA & GOAT CHEESE POPOVERS

In *Volume 1: Eggs*, a Short Stack Editions cook-booklet, Ian Knauer invites home cooks to treat the popover like a blank canvas and experiment with flavors. This is my own version of his maple-bacon popovers. As he notes, never underestimate the magic a couple of eggs can create when mixed with milk and flour (and dulce de leche!). If you don't have pancetta, you can substitute two slices of uncured bacon, cooked crisp and crumbled.

4 ounces pancetta *cubetti* (tiny cubes)

¾ cup whole milk

¼ cup traditional dulce de leche

2 tablespoons fresh goat cheese, softened

2 large eggs

½ teaspoon salt

¼ teaspoon finely ground white pepper

¾ cup all-purpose flour

Leaves from 1 sprig fresh rosemary

Preheat the oven to 375°F. Butter a 6-cup popover pan or 9 cups of a ½-cup muffin tin. In a medium saucepan, cook the pancetta over medium heat until crisp. Transfer to paper towels to drain and let cool.

In a bowl, whisk together the milk and the dulce de leche until combined. Add the goat cheese and mix, then add the eggs, salt and white pepper and whisk until combined. Whisk in the flour until the batter is smooth.

Divide the batter among the popover or muffin cups, and generously sprinkle the tops with the pancetta and a couple of rosemary leaves. Bake until the popovers are puffed and golden brown, about 30 minutes in the muffin tin or 40 minutes in the popover pan. Using a paring knife, cut a slit in the top of each popover to allow steam to escape, then bake for 5 minutes more to cook through. Serve hot.

APRICOT BREAD PUDDING

Although it is a great way to use up day-old bread, I usually buy a loaf specifically for this recipe. As with my French toast, I prefer the sweetness of challah bread, but Italian or French bread are good here, too. As for the cheese toppings, smoked mozzarella lends a creamy savor, but feel free to use whatever you have on hand—ricotta or even whipped cream cheese work just fine. I prepare this the night before, then put it in the oven first thing in the morning as I sip on my *mate*.

4 cups ½-inch bread cubes

2 tablespoons extra-virgin olive oil

3 ounces dried California apricots

1 cup traditional dulce de leche

1 cup heavy cream

6 large eggs

¼ teaspoon freshly ground black pepper

Pinch of salt

½ cup grated smoked fresh mozzarella

Fresh whipped cream, for serving

Fresh mint leaves, for garnish

Preheat the oven to 400°F. Butter a 9-inch cake pan, an 8-inch square pan or 6 individual ramekins. Put the bread cubes on a rimmed baking sheet and drizzle with the olive oil. Bake 10 minutes or until lightly browned and crispy, stirring halfway through baking. Reduce the oven temperature to 350°F. Let the bread cubes cool to room temperature.

While the bread is cooling, in a small saucepan, cover the apricots with water and bring to a boil over high heat. Lower the heat to medium, then cook for 10 minutes more or until soft. Drain the apricots and transfer to a cutting board. Chop them into fine pieces, then mash with a fork. Let cool to room temperature.

In a large bowl, whisk together the dulce de leche and the cream until combined. Add the eggs, pepper and pinch of salt, then whisk in the cooled apricot mash. Stir in the toasted bread cubes and let sit for at least 30 minutes or until the bread is thoroughly saturated.

Pour the bread mixture into the cake pan or divide among the ramekins. Sprinkle the cheese on top and bake for 35 to 40 minutes or until the cheese is bubbling and lightly browned. Let the pudding cool, tented with aluminum foil, for 10 minutes before cutting.

Serve warm with whipped cream and garnish with mint.

The Wisdom of Dorita

MY ABUELA USED TO ALWAYS SAY that if you sing first thing in the morning the day will take care of itself. I would come down to the kitchen and hear, "Oh what a beautiful morning, oh what a beautiful day . . . " Imagine that sung by a five-foot woman with platinum white hair in completely broken English.

I will never forget one morning in the summer of 1981. True to our Argentine fascination with European monarchies, we had all been counting down the days to the royal wedding of Diana and Prince Charles. My brothers, sisters and I camped out in sleeping bags in Dorita and Alfredo's bedroom the night before so we could wake up before to watch it live on TV. We were sound asleep when all of a sudden we heard footsteps climbing the garage apartment stairs. "Oh what a beautiful morning," sang my mom, *"Hoy se casa la Lady Di . . . "* ("Today Lady Di weds").

Abuelo Alfredo, who was right behind her, chuckled, *"De tal palo, tal astilla."* ("Like mother, like daughter.") Alfredo had awakened extra early that morning and prepared *café con leche*, *tostadas* (toast) and sliced *manzanas peladas* (peeled apples) with sides of dulce de leche, *miel* and *mermelada* for each of us. We all piled onto the bed with our coffees; the younger ones with *lagrimas* (warm milk with a "teardrop" of coffee).

"Donde caben dos, caben tres," Dorita said as she scooched over. ("Where there's room for two, there's room for three.")

En la
Merienda

AT TEA TIME, Argentina's cultural fusion comes into focus. For a half hour in late afternoon, between 4:30 and 6:30, everyone stops for *la merienda*, to recharge with coffee and snacks both sweet and savory. Special occasions may call for a formal afternoon tea, but most *meriendas* consist of family, friends or colleagues sitting around the kitchen table or at a local café.

With hours until dinner at 9, 10 or even 11 o'clock, most Argentines need this mid-afternoon caffeine break. All the typical baked breakfast fare makes a second appearance at *la merienda*, only a little grander (overflowing with dulce de leche, jam or cream) and sweeter.

The adults are drinking espresso, a *cortado* (espresso cut with a dab of milk), café con leche, tea or *yerba mate*. Children refer to this time as *la leche*, because they usually drink milk, warmed or cold, with chocolate powder or a tiny "tear" of coffee, which is known as a *lagrima*.

Ordering coffee in a local Argentine café is a memorable cultural experience. You sit at a table and the veteran waiters, *los mozos*, dressed in the traditional penguin suits, arrive with the expectation that you know exactly what you want. Dare to ask for a menu and you'll set off a frenzy or at the very least a lip curled in disgust. *Los mozos* don't write anything down, not even for a party of seven like my family, but miraculously they always appear with the correct order. As their hands fly around the table, effortlessly arranging the little plates so everyone has access, they are happy to bring you up to date on the latest political situation in Argentina, boldly expressing their views.

A favorite aspect of *la merienda* is the *facturas*, beloved miniature pastries that you can find in any *café*, *panadería* or even prepackaged at the local Walmart or its French competitor, Carrefour. *Facturas* are often purchased by the dozen and shared among friends or coworkers. Their origin is European and they are similar to Danish pastries but smaller. They come in a variety of shapes and can be plain or filled with dulce de leche, *crema pastelera* (custard) or *crema chantilly* (whipped cream) and *dulce de membrillo* (quince paste).

To this day, many of the most popular Argentine *facturas* are named with political irony and sarcasm about the country's radical socialist and militant government regimes—*bombas* (bombs) and *cañoncitos con dulce de leche* (little cannons filled with dulce de leche) are two of my favorites.

CHAI LATTE

Dulce de leche is the perfect sweetener for this deliciously smooth latte steeped with chai spices. You can either use a prepared tea blend or create your own chai spice mix. I sometimes substitute almond milk for cow's milk, for a lighter tea with a nutty flavor. If you do not have a milk frother, use whipped cream instead.

1½ cups reduced-fat or whole milk, or almond milk

1 heaping teaspoon chai spice tea blend

1 heaping teaspoon traditional dulce de leche, plus extra for garnish

Dash of cinnamon, for topping

Cinnamon stick, for serving

SPECIAL EQUIPMENT
Tea infuser and milk frother

In a microwave, heat the milk for 1 minute and 30 seconds. (Alternately, heat the milk in a small saucepan over moderate heat just until it reaches a boil.) Pour into a tea glass. Using a tea infuser, add the chai spice tea mix to the milk and stir in 1 heaping teaspoon of dulce de leche. Let steep for 5 minutes.

Froth the latte with a milk frother, then top with a dash of cinnamon. Drizzle dulce de leche and serve hot with a cinnamon stick.

SERVES 4

DULCE DE LECHE HOT CHOCOLATE

Similar to a *submarino* (chocolate bar sunk in hot milk), this is the ultimate comfort drink. The semisweet chocolate provides depth of flavor that isn't typically achieved by using cocoa powder alone. Dulce de leche adds creaminess without making the drink overwhelmingly sweet. Enjoy this with a huge dollop of whipped cream or with plenty of marshmallows.

4 cups milk

¼ cup fine-quality sweet cocoa powder

½ cup traditional dulce de leche

4 ounces semisweet chocolate, chopped

1 cinnamon stick

Marbled Marshmallows (opposite) or whipped cream, for serving

Put the milk and cocoa powder in a saucepan and cook over medium-low heat, whisking to combine. Whisk in the dulce de leche until fully combined, then add the chocolate and whisk until melted.

Add the cinnamon stick and slowly bring to a simmer, whisking frequently so the milk doesn't scorch or form a layer of skin. Serve hot, topped with marshmallows or whipped cream.

MARBLED MARSHMALLOWS

Homemade marshmallows are spectacular when plopped in a cup of hot chocolate, so be sure to try them. They're much lighter and fluffier than the commercial varieties and are extremely easy to make.

¾ ounce (3 packages) unflavored gelatin

1½ cups granulated sugar

1 cup light corn syrup

¼ teaspoon salt

Confectioners' sugar, for dusting

¾ cup confectionary dulce de leche

SPECIAL EQUIPMENT
Candy thermometer

Combine the gelatin and ½ cup cold water in the bowl of a stand mixer fitted with a whisk attachment and whisk on low speed until dissolved. Set aside to soften the gelatin.

In a small saucepan, combine sugar, corn syrup, salt and ½ cup water and cook over medium heat, stirring, until the sugar dissolves. Raise the heat to high and cook, stirring occasionally, until the syrup reaches 240°F, about 10 minutes. Remove the pan from the heat.

With the stand mixer on low speed, slowly pour the hot syrup into the dissolved gelatin. Increase the speed to high and whip until very thick and lukewarm, about 15 minutes. Reduce the speed to the lowest setting and let the marshmallow fall away from the whisk, then turn off the mixer and scrape as much marshmallow as possible from the whisk.

With a sieve, generously dust a 12-by-8-inch nonmetal baking dish with confectioners' sugar. Pour the marshmallow into the pan, smoothing the top with a wet offset spatula. Spread the dulce de leche over the marshmallow in three long parallel lines. Using a table knife or toothpicks, swirl it into the marshmallow in a figure-8 pattern until completely incorporated. Smooth the top again. (If necessary, lightly spray your hands with nonstick cooking spray and tap the marshmallow smooth.) Dust with more confectioners' sugar. Let stand, uncovered, until it dries out, at least 10 hours.

Sprinkle a large cutting board with confectioners' sugar. Using a table knife, gently loosen the marshmallow from the sides of the pan, then turn it out onto the board. Cut the marshmallow into 1-inch squares, occasionally cleaning your knife with hot water. Lightly dust all sides of the marshmallows with more confectioners' sugar.

CAPPUCCINO

In Argentine cafés, cappuccinos and mixed coffee drinks are typically served in a glass so you can see the layers of espresso, milk and foam as they separate. They're also topped with a dash of cinnamon or chocolate, and the waiters always bring an offering of one-bite *alfajores* (traditional sandwich cookies) or *facturas* (pastries).

Unlike the American coffee culture, which mostly centers around in-and-out service, Argentina's coffee scene is substantially mellower and encourages patrons to take a moment to relax and absorb the day before heading back out. Skip the milk and sweeten your brewed coffee with dulce de leche that balances the bitter dark roast espresso bean and offers a velvety, rich finish. In winter, I add a splash of dulce de leche liqueur for extra warmth. In the summer months, we serve these iced and skip the foam.

2 shots espresso, or your favorite coffee

2 teaspoons traditional dulce de leche, or to taste

¼ cup reduced-fat or whole milk, or whipped cream

SPECIAL EQUIPMENT
Espresso machine and milk frother

Brew the espresso or your favorite coffee and pour into a cappuccino or coffee cup. While the coffee is very hot, add the dulce de leche and stir until completely dissolved. Put a small plate or saucer over the cup to keep the coffee hot.

Foam the milk with your espresso machine's steaming wand and add to the top of the coffee, or just add whipped cream.

Yerba Mate

It's almost impossible to write about Argentina's culinary traditions without discussing *yerba mate*. If you shop at natural foods stores, you may be familiar with this bitter herbal tea, which forms the basis of the *mate latte* served in many Starbucks south of the equator. But *mate* is so much more than a drink—it is its own culture in Argentina, Paraguay and Uruguay. It's so popular it even has its own proverbial idiom, *"Calentar el agua para que otro tome mate"* ("Heat the water, only to have another drink the *mate*"), meaning that one person does all the work while another enjoys all the benefits of that work.

Mate can be drunk any time of day, but the most important part of the tradition is that it's drunk communally. *Mate* is as much a social experience as it is a way to quench thirst. In fact, it is such a big part of everyday life that people take their *mate* cup (often a hollow gourd) with them in elaborate carrying cases and drink it everywhere—in their homes, at work, on park benches— and they carry a thermos of hot water to constantly refill the cup.

At *la merienda*, *mate* is accompanied by *bizcochos*, bite-sized biscuits. While usually prepared with hot water, in summer some prefer *mate* as a cold drink called *tereré*, made with iced water or fruit juice. Friends gather in the late afternoon to *tomar mate*. One person assumes the task of server and is designated as the *cebador*, preparing the gourd with dried loose-leaf *yerba*, adding near-to-boiling water and taking the first slow, steady sip from a metal straw lined with a sieve, called a *bombilla*. The *cebador* then begins to pass around the *mate*, refilling it in between turns. The *mate* continues to be passed until you say *gracia*s, which means that you have had your fill.

TORTA DE NARANJA

A traditional Argentine cake that goes well with a cup of tea or *yerba mate* at *la merienda*, *torta de naranja* can be traced back to the Spanish immigration from Andalusia, the southernmost region of Spain that is known to produce some of the world's best oranges.

FOR THE CAKE

½ pound (2 sticks) unsalted butter, at room temperature

2 cups granulated sugar

4 large eggs, at room temperature

⅓ cup grated orange zest (from about 6 oranges)

3 cups all-purpose flour

½ teaspoon baking powder

½ teaspoon baking soda

1 teaspoon salt

¼ cup freshly squeezed orange juice

¾ cup buttermilk, room temperature

1 teaspoon pure vanilla extract

FOR THE DULCE DE LECHE SYRUP

½ cup orange juice

½ cup traditional dulce de leche

SPECIAL EQUIPMENT

Bundt pan

MAKE THE CAKE: Preheat the oven to 350°F. Using a pastry brush, butter the bottom and sides of a bundt pan and sprinkle with flour. In the bowl of a stand mixer fitted with the paddle attachment, cream the butter and sugar for about 5 minutes, or until light and fluffy. With the mixer on medium speed, add the eggs, one at a time, beating after each addition, and add the orange zest.

In a large bowl, sift together the flour, baking powder, baking soda and salt. In another bowl, combine the orange juice, buttermilk and vanilla. Add the flour and buttermilk mixtures alternately to the batter, beginning and ending with the flour. Pour the batter into the prepared bundt pan, smoothing the top. Bake for 50 minutes to 1 hour, or until a skewer inserted in the center comes out clean.

MAKE THE DULCE DE LECHE SYRUP: While the cake bakes, cook the dulce de leche with the orange juice in a small saucepan over low heat and whisk until smooth. When the cake is done, let cool for 10 to 15 minutes, then remove from the pan and cool on a wire rack set over a piece of foil. Spoon orange syrup over the cake and allow to cool completely before slicing and serving.

OR MAKE THE BROWN BUTTER ICING: Melt the butter in a small saucepan over moderately low heat. Stir constantly with a wooden spoon as the butter foams and then turns golden brown, making sure not to let it burn. Once it's brown, remove from the heat and set aside to cool.

This cake keeps, tightly covered, in the refrigerator for up to 1 week or at room temperature for 3 days.

BANANA LICUADO

A smoothie-like blend of milk, fruit and sometimes ice, the *licuado* is a nutritious morning or afternoon drink. In Argentina, you'll see young and old sharing these with a *tostado* (toasted thin sandwich) of ham and cheese around five o'clock in the cafés. My children often make *licuados* for themselves after school, so I keep bananas on hand and stock the freezer with frozen strawberries, raspberries, blueberries and mangoes as well as overripe bananas. I add a teaspoon of chia seeds to thicken and increase nutritional value. Create your own favorite combinations. The sky's the limit here.

2 bananas, fresh or frozen

½ cup traditional dulce de leche

3 cups of cold whole milk, or almond milk

1 teaspoon chia seeds

Put the bananas, dulce de leche, milk and chia seeds in a blender and blend until light and bubbly. Serve immediately.

TOSTADOS DE JAMÓN Y QUESO

(HAM & CREAM CHEESE TOASTED SANDWICHES)

My *abuelo* Alfredo, whose family came from the French Basque region, had a love of cheese, ham and good bread. Most Argentines share his passion, as the culinary influence of their Spanish, Basque, French, Italian and English heritage is strong. As a result, an ubiquitous national dish arose—the *tostado de jamón y queso*. In Argentina, it is commonly made with *jamón crudo or cocido* (cured or cooked ham). This version, made with prosciutto-style cured ham, is a family favorite.

6 very thin slices sandwich bread

Traditional dulce de leche

4 slices cured ham or prosciutto

Whipped cream cheese

Pile the bread slices on a cutting board and remove the crusts with a knife. Divide the pile into two stacks of three pieces each. Working with one stack at a time, thinly spread some dulce de leche on the top of the bottom slice and place a thin layer of prosciutto on top. Thinly spread both sides of the middle piece of bread with whipped cream cheese, and put on top of the bottom slice. Place a second thin layer of prosciutto on top of the middle piece. Thinly spread dulce de leche on the bottom of the top slice and complete the sandwich. Make another sandwich in the same manner.

Place sandwiches on a ridged griddle while gently pressing down with an offset spatula to create grill marks until heated through and lightly toasted. These are equally good served cold.

SÁNDWICHES DE MIGA

con Dulce de Leche

Argentines consume *sándwiches de miga* by the pound. The best I can do to recreate them in the United States is to buy the thinnest white bread I can find, cut off the crusts and play around with the fillings. Although adding dulce de leche is quite a departure from the more common savory *sándwiches de miga*, this is the simplest yet perhaps the most popular variation that I make on a regular basis.

6 very thin slices sandwich bread

Traditional dulce de leche

Unsalted butter, softened

Pile the bread slices on a cutting board and remove the crusts with a knife. Divide the pile into two stacks of three pieces each. Working with one stack at a time, thinly spread some dulce de leche on the top of the bottom slice. Thinly spread both sides of the middle piece of bread with butter, and put on top of the bottom slice. Thinly spread dulce de leche on the bottom of the top slice and complete the sandwich. Make another sandwich in the same manner.

Serve cold or hot as a *tostado*, by grilling on a ridged griddle while gently pressing down with an offset spatula to create grill marks.

Sándwiches de Miga

Instead of making *sándwiches de miga*, or tea sandwiches, from scratch, most Argentines buy them by the pound at their local bakery, where they are piled high in large cardboard cake boxes. Although quite popular for putting hunger at bay at *la merienda*, these paper-thin sandwiches are enjoyed plain or toasted any time of the day. They make a great quick bite at *el almuerzo* (lunch), and finger food for *fiestas de cumpleaños* (birthday parties) or other informal gatherings.

Sándwiches de miga are sold as *simples* (single-layered) or *triples* (double-layered) and are made with a thin white or wheat bread with the crusts removed. The *miga,* or "crumb," primarily refers to the soft inner part of bread and is not to be confused with breadcrumbs. The bread is similar to Pullman style, baked in enormous loaves that are then sliced into extremely thin, long rectangular sheets used specifically for this purpose.

To build the sandwich, the *miga* is lightly brushed with melted butter and filled with thinly sliced *jamón crudo* or *cocido* (cured or cooked ham) in combination with cheese, tomatoes, hearts of palm or lettuce. Egg salad is also popular, paired with tomatoes, green peppers and sometimes other vegetables, even asparagus. The *sándwiches de miga triples* typically will have ham and cheese in one layer and egg salad in the other.

Sándwiches de miga are often compared to the English cucumber sandwich or the Italian *tramezzino*. The *Academia Argentina de Gastronomía* suggests that these sandwiches were introduced into Argentina by immigrants from northern Italy. To the contrary, the Buenos Aires newspaper *Clarín* claims the *sándwich de miga* was actually invented by local bakers at the Confitería Ideal—a time-honored Buenos Aires café and dance hall—for a group of homesick British engineers who used to frequent their establishment during the early part of the twentieth century. One thing is for sure—they are still as sought after today as they were back then.

COCADAS

The South American version of the coconut macaroon *cocadas* are particularly popular in Argentina, Brazil, Chile, Colombia, Venezuela and México. Gastón's grandmother Elsa loved *cocadas*. She would make trays and trays of delicately bite-sized macaroons and serve them when she invited family and friends for an afternoon *merienda*. This is a gluten-free recipe that is super tasty and easy to make. I like to keep half of the *cocadas* plain and dip the remainder in melted semisweet chocolate.

1 (14-ounce) can sweetened condensed milk

⅓ cup traditional dulce de leche

1 teaspoon pure vanilla extract

4¼ cups unsweetened shredded coconut

2 extra-large egg whites, at room temperature

¼ teaspoon salt

1 cup semisweet chocolate chips, or 1 (4-ounce) bar semisweet chocolate, melted

Preheat the oven to 325°F. Line two baking sheets with parchment paper. In a large bowl, whisk together the condensed milk, dulce de leche and vanilla. Stir in the coconut.

In a mixing bowl, beat the egg whites and salt on high speed with an electric mixer until medium-firm peaks form. Carefully fold the egg whites into the coconut mixture. Using an ice cream scoop or 2 spoons, drop ¼-cup mounds of the mixture onto the baking sheets at least ½ inch apart. Bake for 25 to 30 minutes until golden brown. Let the *cocadas* cool slightly on the baking sheets until they are warm to the touch, then transfer to a cooling rack to cool completely.

When the *cocadas* are completely cool, melt the chocolate in a double boiler, stirring constantly, until melted. Line the baking sheet with a clean sheet of parchment paper. Dip the bottom of the *cocadas* into the chocolate to coat, then return them to the baking sheet and refrigerate until the chocolate is set, about 1 hour. The *cocadas* keep, in an airtight container at room temperature, up to 5 days.

The Wisdom of Dorita

As a child, Gastón's mom, Graciela, unfailingly served him and his five siblings *la merienda* every day at *las cinco y pico* (5 o'clockish). No matter where they were, or what they were doing, when they heard her calling, they'd drop everything and come in to drink their *leche chocolatada*.

My grandma Dorita also was a faithful *meriendera*, and some of my favorite moments with her were at this time of day, especially in her later years. Despite a generalized listlessness she experienced while in her nineties, *merienda* time would suddenly affect Dorita's loquacious spirit.

We always started with large cups of hot *café con leche*. She would slowly stir sweetener into her mug, her long thin fingers with perfectly polished fingernails pushing the spoon round and round as she began to eye a large plate of *facturas* (pastries) in the middle of the table, mulling over which to choose first. A fan of *dulce con salado* (sweet and salty) myself, I usually opted for the *sándwiches de miga* (paper-thin tea sandwiches).

Dorita would slowly reach over and choose a *pañuelito de grasa* (a pastry in the form of a folded handkerchief) filled with dulce de leche, daintily lifting it up by one end and gently dipping the other end into the warm coffee. And with that first bite, Dorita would suddenly become the *abuela charlatana* (chatty grandmother) I had always been accustomed to, filled with stories and questions.

BOMBAS

con Chocolate Bariloche

Bombas are a classic Argentine *factura* served at tea time; they are sometimes filled with *crema pastelera* (pastry cream) instead. My mother-in-law, Graciela, is an expert at these. For formal occasions, she presents them as a towering cake by stacking them into a large cone, which she then drizzles with *chocolate Bariloche*—a silky smooth ganache named after Argentina's Patagonian city San Carlos de Bariloche.

Popular with tourists, Bariloche is known for three things: skiing, fly fishing and chocolate shops. *Chocolate Bariloche* is made with butter, dulce de leche and dark chocolate and is used as a glaze poured over cakes or as a frosting after it's been allowed to cool. It can also be poured over ice cream.

FOR THE PASTRY PUFFS

½ cup (1 stick) unsalted butter

1 dash of salt

1 cup all-purpose flour

4 large eggs

FOR THE FILLING

1½ cups confectionary dulce de leche

FOR THE CHOCOLATE BARILOCHE GLAZE

1 cup (2 sticks) unsalted butter, softened

6 ounces dark chocolate, chopped

2 to 3 heaping tablespoons confectionary or traditional dulce de leche

SPECIAL EQUIPMENT

Pastry bag and a very thin tip

MAKE THE PASTRY PUFFS: Preheat the oven to 350°F. Lightly grease two large baking sheets with nonstick cooking spray. In a medium pot, combine 1 cup water, the butter and salt and bring just to a boil over medium-high heat. Lower the heat to a simmer, then slowly add the flour, stirring quickly with a wooden spoon, and simmer for about 10 minutes to cook through. Remove the pan from the heat and let cool for 5 minutes.

Add the eggs, one at a time, stirring quickly until the batter is silky smooth. After adding the first egg, the mixture may separate, but continue stirring and it will come together again.

Form balls of dough, one at a time, by rolling a teaspoonful of the dough between the palms of your hands and then placing them one inch apart on the baking sheets. Bake for 25 to 30 minutes or until golden brown. Let the puffs cool on the baking sheets for at least 25 minutes.

FILL THE BOMBAS: When the puffs are completely cool, fit a pastry bag with a very thin tip, fill it with confectionary dulce de leche and pipe it into the puffs. (Alternatively, you can either use a squeeze bottle

CONTINUED

or you can use a paring knife to make an incision in each puff, taking care not to slice all of the way through, and then carefully spoon in the filling.) Transfer to a serving platter.

MAKE THE CHOCOLATE BARILOCHE GLAZE: In a medium saucepan, combine the butter, chocolate and confectionary or traditional dulce de leche and cook over low heat, stirring constantly until well combined and a velvety consistency is reached. Remove the pan from the heat and let cool for 5 minutes. The glaze will set as it cools, so don't let it cool completely.

Drizzle the glaze over the *bombas* and serve immediately.

TO MAKE A HOLLOW CONE OF BOMBAS: Form a round base of 10 to 12 of the larger *bombas*, then add more layer by layer to form a cone shape with the smaller ones on the top. You can use the glaze to stick them together and secure the ones on top with wooden toothpicks.

VARIATION: Instead of the chocolate topping, Graciela sometimes envelops the *bombas* in a nest of *hilos de caramel* (caramel strings). For the caramel, place 2 cups granulated sugar and ½ cup water in a shallow saucepan and stir to combine. Cover and cook over medium heat until the sugar turns a light amber, about 15 to 20 minutes. Remove from heat and allow to cool slightly until caramel is the consistency of honey. With a spoon, drizzle thin strings of caramel around the cone.

You can also sprinkle the filled *bombas* with confectioners' sugar.

BOMBAS RELLENAS
con Roquefort

Graciela always makes extra *bombas* and sets them aside, filling them with savory flavors to serve at *la merienda* or later in the evening at *la picada*. A *picada* (page 99) is a wonderful Argentinian tradition of serving artfully arranged finger foods for everyone to share. This recipe calls for Roquefort, as Argentines love this cheese in *picadas* and meal preparations—it is even a common pizza topping—but any crumbly cheese, such as Gorgonzola, may be substituted.

FOR THE PASTRY PUFFS

½ cup (1 stick) unsalted butter

1 dash of salt

1 cup all-purpose flour

4 large eggs

FOR THE FILLING

¼ cup Roquefort cheese, softened and cut into small pieces

3 teaspoons heavy cream

1 teaspoon bourbon whiskey

¾ cup confectionary dulce de leche

MAKE THE BOMBAS: Preheat the oven to 350°F. Lightly grease two large baking sheets with nonstick cooking spray. In a medium pot, combine 1 cup water, the butter and salt and bring just to a boil over medium-high heat. Lower the heat to a simmer, then slowly add the flour, stirring quickly with a wooden spoon, and simmer for about 10 minutes to cook through. Remove the pan from the heat and let cool for 5 minutes.

Add the eggs, one at a time, stirring quickly until the batter is silky smooth. After adding the first egg, the mixture may separate, but continue stirring and it will come together again.

Form balls of dough, one at a time, by rolling a teaspoonful of the dough between the palms of your hands. Place the balls 1 inch apart on the baking sheets and bake for 25 to 30 minutes or until golden brown. Let the puffs cool on the baking sheets for at least 25 minutes.

MAKE THE FILLING: In a small saucepan, combine the Roquefort cheese and cream over medium-low heat, stirring constantly, just until a creamy consistency is achieved, then immediately remove the pan from the heat. Stir in the bourbon, stirring until combined, then stir in the confectionary dulce de leche until well combined. Let the filling cool for about 30 minutes.

Using a paring knife, make an incision in each pastry, taking care not to slice all the way through, and carefully spoon in the filling. Transfer the *bombas* to a platter and serve immediately.

VARIATION: You can turn these *bombas* into delicious cocktail hour nibbles by filling them with *queso de cabra* (goat cheese) and pancetta. For the filling: In a medium saucepan, cook 4 ounces of chopped pancetta over medium heat until crisp. Transfer to paper towels to drain and let cool. In a medium mixing bowl, combine the goat cheese and cooled pancetta, then beat them together on high speed with an electric mixer until light and fluffy. Add salt, pepper and flat-leaf parsley to taste. Using a paring knife, make an incision in each pastry, taking care not to slice all of the way through, and carefully spoon in the filling.

"ROLL THE DICE" COOKIES

I make these cookies for my family on our occasional game nights, when we use them as poker chips ranging from $1 to $6. Who says you can't play with your food? These one-bite treats are simple to make if you freehand the squares with a pizza cutter and throw the idea of perfection out the window. Once you have a plate of 30 little dice cookies on a table, no one will notice that they aren't perfectly shaped. (Of course, you could also invest in a square cookie cutter, which I just might do one of these days.)

FOR THE CHOCOLATE COOKIE DOUGH

2½ cups all-purpose flour

½ cup unsweetened cocoa powder

½ cup confectioners' sugar

½ teaspoon salt

1 cup (2 sticks) cold unsalted butter, cut into small cubes

1 large egg

1 large egg yolk

FOR THE FILLING

½ cup confectionary dulce de leche

FOR THE "DOTS"

6 ounces melting wafers

SPECIAL EQUIPMENT

Pastry bag, a very small round tip and a 1-inch square cookie cutter (all optional)

MAKE THE COOKIE DOUGH: In a bowl, whisk together the flour, cocoa powder, confectioners' sugar and salt until well blended. With two knives, cut in the butter until pea-sized lumps form. Add the egg and egg yolk and mix just until a dough starts to form. (Alternatively, you can make the dough in a food processor: Put the flour, cocoa powder, confectioners' sugar and salt in the bowl of the processor, add the butter, cut into small cubes, and pulse until pea-sized lumps form. Add the whole egg and egg yolk and pulse just until a ball starts to form.)

Turn out the dough onto a clean floured surface and knead minimally, just to incorporate any extra flour and cocoa powder. Form the dough into a disk and let the dough rest in the refrigerator, wrapped in plastic wrap, for at least 30 minutes and up to 2 days.

Preheat the oven to 375°F. Line a baking sheet with parchment paper. On a clean lightly floured surface, roll the dough into a ¼-inch-thick rectangle. Using a pizza cutter, cut the dough into 1-inch squares and place on the baking sheet. Bake for 7 minutes, or until the edges become slightly crisp. Let cool completely on the baking sheet.

FILL THE COOKIES: Put the dulce de leche into a pastry bag fitted with a small round tip, or put into a sealable plastic bag and cut off a corner. Working with three cookie squares to form each "dice," pipe a dollop of dulce de leche in the middle of the bottom cookie. Place the second cookie on top, and pipe a dollop of dulce de leche in the middle.

CONTINUED

Place the third cookie on top. Set aside and let set. Make more "dice" in the same manner with all the remaining cookies.

ADD THE "DOTS" TO COMPLETE THE "DICE": In a double boiler, melt the white chocolate wafers and let cool completely. When cool, put the white chocolate into a pastry bag fitted with a small round tip and pipe dots onto the cookies to make dice ranging from "1" to "6."

ALFAJORES

The beloved national Argentine cookie is made of two soft, crumbly halves with dulce de leche, chocolate or local jams in the middle. Some are cake-like, others are buttery and some, like these *alfajores de maicena*, are made with cornstarch. The equal parts cornstarch to butter, sugar and flour create a memorably tender cookie.

My grandparents always made sure to bring boxes of *alfajores* Havanna, a popular brand from Mar del Plata (a coastal city south of Buenos Aires), when they visited from Argentina. They brought *alfajores de fruta* filled with *mermelada de membrillo* (quince jam) and bathed in meringue for my mom, *alfajores de café* (chocolate-covered *alfajores* filled with coffee-flavored dulce de leche) for my dad and a mixture of *alfajores de dulce de leche* bathed in dark chocolate and white meringue for the kids.

In Argentina, *alfajores* are enjoyed with coffee or tea in the morning, as an afternoon snack or after dinner for a decadent dessert. It is common for Argentine kids to scrounge up *monedas* (coins) and pop into their neighborhood *kiosko* (small candy and news store) to pick up their favorite *alfajor*. I prefer to make them bite-size; sometimes that little bit is all you need for an afternoon pick-me-up.

FOR THE COOKIES

2 cups all-purpose flour

2 cups cornstarch

2 teaspoons baking powder

½ teaspoon baking soda

17 tablespoons (2 sticks plus 1 tablespoon) unsalted butter, softened

¾ cup of granulated sugar

3 large egg yolks

1 teaspoon vanilla extract

1 teaspoon lemon zest

FOR THE FILLING

1½ cups confectionary dulce de leche

1 cup shredded coconut

In a large bowl, whisk together the flour, cornstarch, baking powder and baking soda. Set aside.

In a mixing bowl, blend together the butter and sugar on medium speed with an electric mixer until combined, then add the egg yolks, one at a time, and blend until pale yellow. Reduce the speed to low, and mix in the vanilla extract and the lemon zest until well combined. Gradually add the reserved flour mixture, about one-quarter of the mixture at a time until completely combined, making sure each addition is fully incorporated before adding the next. Form the dough into a ball and refrigerate, wrapped in plastic wrap, for 30 minutes.

While the dough chills, preheat the oven to 375°F. Line a baking sheet with parchment paper. When the dough is chilled, dust a work surface with flour and roll out the dough evenly to a ¼ inch thickness. With a small or large round cookie cutter, cut out as many cookies as possible

CONTINUED

Pastry bag, a large pastry tip and a 1½-inch round cookie cutter or a 3-inch round cookie cutter

and place them on the baking sheet ½ inch apart. Roll out any dough scraps and cut out more cookies in the same manner, transferring them to the baking sheet. (You should have a total of 24 large rounds or 48 small rounds.)

Bake the larger cookies for 13 to 15 minutes or the bite-size cookies for 9 to 10 minutes until the edges are golden. Remove from oven and slide the parchment with the cookies on it onto a cooling rack.

FILL THE COOLED COOKIES: Fit a pastry bag with a large tip, fill it with dulce de leche and carefully spread an even layer of dulce de leche on the bottom side of a cookie and sandwich with the bottom of another cookie. (Note: These cookies are very crumbly to the touch, so handle with care and always fill them using a pastry bag fitted with a large tip.)

ADD THE COCONUT TOPPING: Put the coconut in a shallow bowl. Using a knife, spread additional dulce de leche over the sides of the sandwiched cookies, then roll in the coconut, making sure to cover all sides.

For white meringue topping called baño blanco

Combine 2 cups granulated sugar with ½ cup of water in a small saucepan and heat over medium-high heat until it reaches a boil. Stir to dissolve the sugar in the water, and continue to boil until the sugar syrup thickens slightly but is not caramelized, about ten minutes. (A spoonful of it should be thick enough to create a thread of syrup.)

Meanwhile, in a medium mixing bowl, beat 2 egg whites on medium-high speed with an electric mixer until slightly stiff, white and fluffy, 3 to 5 minutes. When the sugar syrup is the right consistency, slowly drizzle it into the bowl with the egg whites, beating continuously. You will have a glossy creamy meringue. It shouldn't be stiff, since you want to be able to paint it on.

Using a pastry brush, spread the meringue onto the outside of the *alfajores*. Set on a cookie sheet or work surface lined with parchment paper and let dry for several hours or overnight. The *baño blanco* will eventually form a dry crust.

For decadent alfajores dipped in chocolate glaze

In a double boiler over medium heat, stir together 3 ounces of coarsely chopped bittersweet chocolate, 4 tablespoons unsalted butter and 2 teaspoons of light corn syrup until combined. Let the mixture cool, then carefully dunk the cookies into the glaze with your fingers. Allow the *alfajores* to set for at least 30 minutes.

Alfajores in Argentina

Most Spanish words beginning with "*al*" have Arabic roots, and this beloved dulce de leche sandwich cookie is no exception. Its origin can be traced back to the Moorish occupation of Andalusia, Spain, and the great Mediterranean culinary traditions.

There are many versions of *alfajores*, and each Argentine province puts its own stamp on the cookie. If you are traveling in the hills of Córdoba, or the city of Bariloche in the southern Andes, or visiting the beaches in Mar del Plata, it's essential to buy a few boxes of regional *alfajores* for family or friends back home. My mom spent her childhood in the wine country of Mendoza and was partial to that regional interpretation of the *alfajor*—a cake-like cookie with a hint of anise, filled with dulce de leche and coated with a *baño blanco*, or meringue.

Throughout Argentina, however, classic *alfajores* are filled with dulce de leche and either rolled in coconut, dipped in chocolate or simply dusted with confectioners' sugar. More recent innovations include cookies with multiple layers, a greater variety of fillings and toppings, and gluten-free *alfajores* made with rice flour.

OATMEAL CHOCOLATE CHIP COOKIES

Who doesn't love chocolate chip cookies? They are so easy to make and their aroma can lighten the mood in any household. These are packed with oatmeal; it creates a much heartier cookie that holds up when dipped in a glass of cold milk.

2¼ cups all-purpose flour

1 teaspoon baking soda

½ teaspoon salt

1 cup (2 sticks) unsalted butter, softened

¾ cup traditional dulce de leche

¾ cup brown sugar, packed

2 teaspoons pure vanilla extract

2 large eggs

3 cups old-fashioned oats

10 ounces 60% cacao bittersweet chocolate chips

Preheat the oven to 375°F. Line two large baking sheets with parchment. In a large bowl, stir together the flour, baking soda and salt.

In a large bowl, beat the butter, dulce de leche and brown sugar at medium speed with an electric mixer until fluffy and light in color. Reduce the speed to low and add the vanilla and eggs, one at a time, mixing until incorporated. Gradually add the flour mixture and mix until combined well. Stir in the oats and chocolate chips.

Using two spoons, drop 1-tablespoon mounds of dough at least 1 inch apart onto the baking sheets. Bake 9 to 10 minutes or until golden brown. While the cookies are still warm, transfer to wire racks to cool.

SHORTBREAD COOKIES

This unassuming cookie is Gastón's favorite. He loves their buttery texture and the fact that they are not too sweet. I always bake one batch for him and another for the children, as he's capable of downing a plate of them in one sitting. Shortbread, perfectly simple and delicious with coffee or tea, holds up well in the cookie jar. The optional addition of chocolate chips or peppermint bits makes them a bit more special.

1⅓ cups unsalted butter, cold

¾ cup granulated sugar

¾ cup confectionary dulce de leche

2 teaspoons of pure vanilla extract

2½ cups self-rising flour

1 tablespoon baking powder

Small chocolate chips or peppermint bits, if desired

Confectioners' sugar, to decorate

Preheat the oven to 350°F. In a food processor, process the butter, sugar and dulce de leche until creamy. Add the vanilla extract and pulse once or twice to combine.

Transfer the mixture to a large mixing bowl. With a wooden spoon, slowly fold in the flour and the baking powder until just blended. If desired, gently stir in the chocolate chips or peppermint bits. Turn out the dough onto a work surface, and with your hands, gently roll it into a 14-inch log, taking care not to overwork the dough. Refrigerate the log, wrapped in plastic wrap, for 30 minutes.

Transfer the chilled log to a work surface and slice into about 30 pieces. With the palms of your hands, roll each piece into a ball and place about 1 inch apart on a large baking sheet lined with parchment. Using a fork, form a crisscross pattern on the top of each ball.

Bake for 12 to 14 minutes until the edges are golden brown. Transfer the cookies to a wire rack and let cool. Dust with confectioners' sugar before serving.

DULCE DE LECHE CHOCOLATE EMPANADAS

Empanadas are savory hand pies filled with meat or ham and cheese, and they are very popular in our home. I almost always have *tapas* (the round dough discs) left over, and that is how I first came to make dulce de leche *empanadas*. I stuff the last *tapas* with dulce de leche and brie or sliced bananas, and my boys love them. They remind me of my siblings and me when we were young: my Dad and my brother, Olito, had voracious appetites, especially for Argentine fare. Any time Dorita made *empanadas*, she would hide a plate for us girls to ensure we got our fair share. Whenever I walked into our kitchen panicking that the *empanadas* were gone, Dorita would pull a covered dish from the strangest hiding places, like out of a drawer or the microwave. I always loved her for this.

Because this *empanada* variation is on the sweeter side, I like to make them bite-sized. While baking, some of the dulce de leche may leak, so I keep a small tub of it with a knife on the table in case anyone wants to refill theirs with a bit more before taking that second bite. I finish with a bit of sea salt.

3 cups all-purpose flour

¾ cup unsweetened cocoa powder

¼ cup granulated sugar

Pinch of salt

1 cup (2 sticks) unsalted butter, room temperature, cut into cubes

3 large eggs, divided

4 to 6 tablespoons whole milk

4 cups confectionary dulce de leche

Sea salt, to sprinkle on top

SPECIAL EQUIPMENT
1½-inch or 3-inch round cookie cutter

Put the flour, cocoa powder, sugar and salt in a large bowl and stir together until combined. With two knives, cut the butter into the flour.

Add 2 eggs, one at a time, stirring well after each addition, until well combined. Add 4 tablespoons of the milk and continue to stir just until a dough begins to form.

Turn out the dough onto a floured surface and knead, adding more milk if necessary, one tablespoon at a time, until well combined and smooth. Form the dough into two balls, flatten into thick rounds, and refrigerate, wrapped in plastic, for at least 30 minutes and up to 1 day.

On a lightly floured surface, use a rolling pin to stretch the dough into a thin sheet about ¼ inch thick. Using a 1½-inch or 3-inch round cookie cutter, cut the dough into rounds. The rounds can be filled immediately or layered with wax paper and kept in a sealable plastic bag in the

CONTINUED

refrigerator for up to 3 days or the freezer for 1 month.

Preheat the oven to 375°F. Lightly grease two baking sheets with nonstick cooking spray. Prepare a small bowl of cold water. On a work surface, arrange three or four empanada rounds about an inch apart. Place a spoonful of dulce de leche in the center of each round. Dip two fingers into the water and wet the edge of each round, then fold the rounds in half over the dulce de leche, sealing the edges gently with your fingers. Use the tip of a fork to further seal the edges. Arrange the empanadas on the baking sheets. Continue to fill and form the remaining empanadas in the same manner.

In a small bowl, whisk the remaining egg with 1 tablespoon water until frothy. Lightly brush the tops of the empanadas with the egg wash and sprinkle with a pinch of sea salt. Bake for 15 to 20 minutes until the dough is lightly browned and cooked through (the exact time will vary according to the size of the empanadas). Serve warm.

VARIATION: When I don't have confectionary dulce de leche on hand, I use mascarpone cheese to thicken traditional dulce de leche. For the filling, combine 2½ cups mascarpone with 1½ cups traditional dulce de leche. This variation is a little less sweet but equally delicious.

MAKES 16 BROWNIES

DOUBLE-CHOCOLATE BROWNIES

Since I was a child, brownies have been my ultimate indulgence. I used to "bake" them only to eat the batter. Now I spread a thin layer of dulce de leche on top, and it seeps deliciously into the batter as they bake, adding an extra gooeyness to the cake-like batter. This trick is also great for gluten-free boxed brownie mixes, as it makes them very moist.

26 tablespoons (3 sticks plus 2 tablespoons) unsalted butter

12 ounces fine-quality bittersweet chocolate

6 large eggs

1¼ cups granulated sugar

1 tablespoon pure vanilla extract

1½ cups plus 2 tablespoons all-purpose flour

1 teaspoon salt

½ cup semisweet chocolate chips, buttons or morsels

½ cup traditional dulce de leche

Preheat the oven to 350°F. Butter and flour a 13-by-9-by-2-inch baking pan and line the bottom with parchment paper. In a large heavy saucepan over low heat, melt the butter and bittersweet chocolate together, stirring constantly until combined. Set aside to cool slightly.

Meanwhile, in a bowl or large measuring cup, beat the eggs with the sugar and vanilla.

When the chocolate mixture is slightly cooled, whisk the egg mixture into the chocolate mixture and fold in the flour and salt. Whisk the mixture until smooth, about 1 minute. Stir in the chocolate chips.

Scrape and pour the brownie mixture into the baking pan, smoothing the top with a spatula. With a clean spatula, spread the dulce de leche over the top in three long parallel lines; using two toothpicks, swirl it evenly over the surface.

Bake for 35 to 40 minutes or until the top dries to a slightly paler brown speckle while the middle remains dark, dense and gooey. Turn off the oven, open the door slightly, and let the brownies cool in the oven for 10 minutes to make sure the center is set.

93
EN LA MERIENDA

ARROZ CON LECHE CRIOLLO

Rice pudding is one of the most beloved desserts in the Latin world and a simple taste of childhood. It is supreme comfort food that is simple to make. Dorita always seemed to have a piping hot pot of *arroz con leche* waiting for us when we arrived home from school on a rainy cold afternoon. While the pudding is delicious hot, the flavor gets better and better as the rice has time to settle. Serve this plain or with your favorite toppings.

6 cups whole milk

1 cup basmati rice

¾ cup traditional dulce de leche

1 teaspoon pure vanilla extract

Ground cinnamon or additional dulce de leche, for topping hot pudding

Unsweetened coconut, mini chocolate chips or ½ teaspoon lemon zest, for mixing into cooled pudding

Combine the milk, rice, dulce de leche and vanilla extract in a medium heavy saucepan and bring just to a boil over medium-high heat, stirring constantly. Reduce the heat to low and continue to cook, uncovered, stirring constantly until the mixture is thick, about 20 to 30 minutes.

Transfer the pudding to a serving bowl and let cool at least 10 minutes to allow the rice to thicken. If serving warm, dust the top with ground cinnamon or drizzle with dulce de leche. If serving cold (our preference), refrigerate once cool, covered with plastic wrap, for at least 30 minutes, then mix in mini chocolate chips or lemon zest. The pudding keeps in the refrigerator for up to 3 days.

ROSQUITOS

Dorita used to make these little baked doughnuts with leftover dough from her *tartas* (pies). We would all fight over *rosquitos*, even when there was an entire *tarta* in front of us to be eaten. She finally got so fed up that she would forego the *tarta* and only make the *rosquitos*. They are similar to scones and can be dunked in coffee, tea or milk. Or spread them with more dulce de leche, butter or jelly of your choice (they are delicious with a bit of orange marmalade).

2 to 2½ cups unbleached all-purpose flour

1 whole large egg

1 large egg yolk

1 cup granulated sugar

½ cup cold unsalted butter, cut into cubes

¼ cup plus 1 teaspoon traditional dulce de leche

Pinch of salt

Extra flour, for dusting

Put the flour, whole egg and egg yolk, sugar, butter, dulce de leche and salt into a food processor and pulse until pea-size balls form. Turn out the dough onto a work surface.

With floured hands, knead just until a smooth consistency is formed, adding a bit more dulce de leche if necessary. Lightly flour the top of the dough and form into a round. Put the dough, wrapped in plastic, on a baking sheet and refrigerate for 30 minutes. The dough can be used immediately or kept in the refrigerator for up to 1 day.

Preheat the oven to 325°F. Lightly coat a baking sheet with nonstick cooking spray. Using a ¼ cup measuring cup, divide dough evenly into 12 balls. With floured hands, form each ball into a 5-inch log, then connect the ends to form a doughnut and transfer to the baking sheet. Form more doughnuts in the same manner with the remaining balls, placing the doughnuts 1 inch apart on the sheet. Bake for 17 to 20 minutes until golden brown. While the doughnuts are still warm, transfer to racks to cool completely.

CHURROS

FILLED WITH DULCE DE LECHE

Crunchy on the outside and soft on the inside, *churros* are Argentine street food at its best. Street vendors fry them up fresh, piping the batter directly into the hot oil, and sell them plain or filled with dulce de leche or *crema pastelera* (pastry cream). If you don't have time to fill your *churros*, warm up some hot chocolate or dulce de leche for dipping. Simplicity is the key to making the perfect *churro*—the batter requires equal parts water and flour and a good strong arm to quickly incorporate the two. If you want to make authentic *churros*, you'll need to find a 13-millimeter pastry star tip.

⅓ cup cold unsalted butter, cut into cubes

4 cups all-purpose flour, sifted

Grated zest of 2 oranges

Canola oil for deep frying

2 cups dulce de leche

2 tablespoons ground cinnamon

1⅓ cups granulated sugar

SPECIAL EQUIPMENT (OPTIONAL):
2 pastry bags, a jumbo 13-millimeter star tip and a small pointed tip, and a candy thermometer

Put the butter and 4 cups of water into a large saucepan and heat gently over low heat, stirring constantly, until the butter melts. Increase the heat to medium-high and bring just to a rolling boil. Add the flour all at once, stirring vigorously with a wooden spoon, then reduce the heat to low and continue to cook the dough, stirring until it pulls away from the side of the pan and forms a ball, about 1 minute. Remove the pan from the heat and let cool for 5 minutes, then mix in the orange zest.

Spoon the dough into a pastry bag fitted with a jumbo 13-millimeter star tip. (If you do not have a pastry bag, use a heavy plastic bag and cut a ½-inch slit at one corner. You will not have the classic ridged exterior that *churros* are known for, but the taste will be the same.)

In a large saucepan, heat 6 inches of oil over medium heat until it reaches 360°F on a candy thermometer. (If you do not have a thermometer, you can test to see whether the oil is hot enough by adding a drop of the dough mixture; if it bubbles and immediately rises to the top, the oil is sufficiently hot.) Gently pipe a 6-inch length of dough into the oil and sweep off the dough with your finger. Pipe a few more pieces of dough. Do not crowd the pan. Deep-fry the *churros*, turning halfway through frying with a slotted spoon, for 4 minutes total or until crisp, golden brown and cooked through. Remove with the slotted spoon and drain on paper towels. Fry and drain the remaining dough in batches in the same manner.

Meanwhile, spoon the dulce de leche into a second piping bag fitted with a smaller pointed tip and set aside. In a large bowl, stir together the cinnamon and sugar and set aside.

When all the *churros* are cool to the touch, with a paring knife carefully make a lengthwise incision along each one, taking care not to cut all the way through. Carefully pipe dulce de leche into the slit from one end to the other, then toss the filled *churros* in the cinnamon mixture. Serve immediately.

BUÑUELOS

WITH BROWN VELVET GLAZE

Basically a fried dough ball that you may know as *zeppole*, the *buñuelo* is another popular snack in Argentina, and the dough is very similar to that of a *churro*. If you are making it at home, it's an easy way to get that fried doughnut taste, especially if you don't have the patience or equipment to make *churros* or you just feel like free-styling the dough.

FOR THE DOUGH

½ cup (1 stick) unsalted butter

¼ teaspoon salt

¾ cup granulated sugar, divided

1 cup all-purpose flour

4 large eggs

2 tablespoons orange zest, divided

Canola oil, for frying

FOR THE BROWN VELVET GLAZE

½ cup heavy whipping cream

6 ounces of 60% cacao chocolate, coarsely chopped

¼ cup (½ stick) unsalted butter, at room temperature

¼ cup traditional dulce de leche

SPECIAL EQUIPMENT

Candy thermometer

MAKE THE DOUGH: In a medium saucepan, combine the butter, salt, ¼ cup sugar and ½ cup water and bring to a boil over medium heat. Remove the pan from the heat and stir in the flour all at once until combined. Return the pan to low heat and stir continuously until the mixture forms a ball, about 4 minutes.

Transfer the dough to a mixing bowl and using an electric handheld mixer on low speed, add the eggs, one at a time, incorporating each egg completely before adding the next. Add 1 tablespoon of the orange zest and beat until smooth.

In another bowl, combine the remaining ½ cup sugar with the remaining tablespoon orange zest and set aside.

In a large saucepan, heat 2 inches of oil over medium-high heat until it reaches 360°F on a candy thermometer. (If you do not have a thermometer, you can test to see whether the oil is hot enough by adding a drop of the dough; if it bubbles and immediately rises to the top, the oil is sufficiently hot.) Using a small ice-cream scoop or 2 small spoons, carefully drop three or four 1-tablespoon mounds of dough into the hot oil. Do not crowd the pan. Fry the *buñuelos*, turning them once or twice with a slotted spoon, about 5 minutes until golden and puffed up. Transfer with the slotted spoon to the orange sugar and toss to coat, then put on a serving platter. Continue to fry and coat the remaining dough in the same manner.

WHILE FRYING THE LAST BATCH, PREPARE THE GLAZE: In a small saucepan, heat the cream over low heat until bubbles form around edges of the pan, then pour into a large heatproof bowl and let cool for 1 minute. Add the chocolate all at once and stir together with a rubber spatula. Put the bowl over a pan with simmering (not steaming) water and stir constantly until the chocolate is completely melted. Add the butter in small chunks, stirring until incorporated, then pour the glaze through a sieve into a small bowl to obtain a velvety shine.

Serve immediately as a dip for the *buñuelos*. As the glaze cools, it will thicken. If necessary, reheat in a metal bowl over a double boiler. As the glaze warms through, it will turn glossy once again.

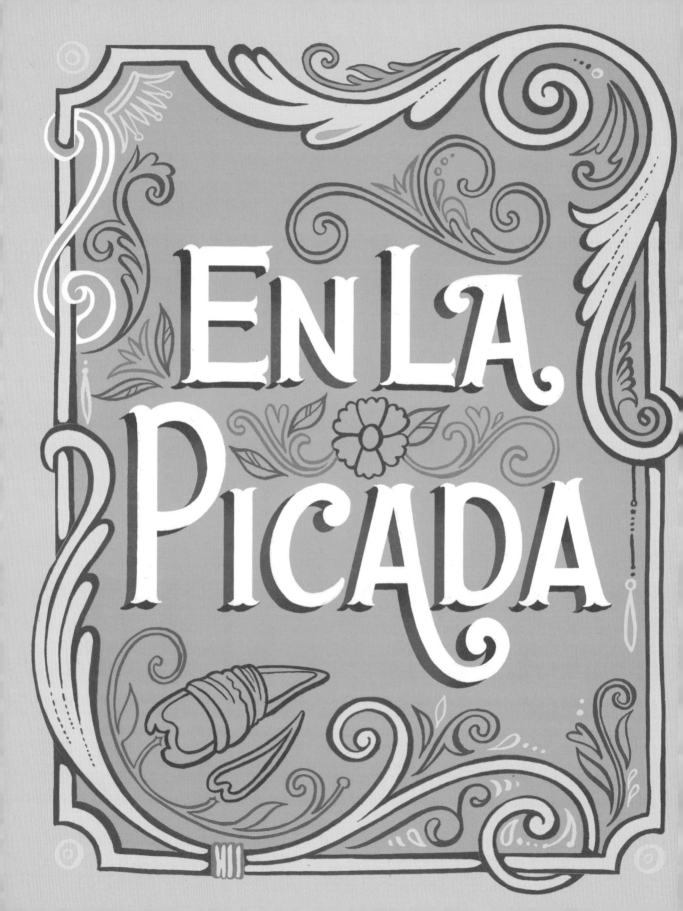

AN ENSEMBLE of artfully arranged finger foods to share while drinking red wine, vermouth or beer, the *picada* reflects the strong European influence evident in many Argentine food traditions; it's our version of the Italian antipasto and the Spanish tapas custom. The ingredients for a *picada* can be lavish and precisely arrayed, or a simpler, more inventive spread may be composed to use up leftovers.

Picada (which comes from the Spanish *picar*, "to pick") is often served as an appetizer, especially before a lengthy weekend *asado*, while the *asador* oversees the grilling of the meat. But it can also be a casual meal in itself, or you can go the *picada* route for *la merienda* and swap savory snacks for sweet. Whenever you have it, it feels like a treat.

Outside of the home, a *picada* may be shared in bars, cafés, *parrillas* (grill restaurants) or *bodegónes* (simple neighborhood eateries run by and for immigrants, traditionally of Spanish or Italian descent). Served on wooden platters or a large cutting board in rustic *campo* style, or as a *surtido* of small plates, the offerings are meant to be varied and stimulating to the appetite.

CONTINUED

Fiambres are essential to any *picada*. They include smoked and cured cold cuts, some neatly rolled up into cylinders or wrapped around a bread stick: *jamón cocido* (cooked ham), *jamón crudo* (cured ham, prosciutto style), *salamín* (dried and cured chorizo, sopressata style) or *mortadella* (bologna), along with other *ahumados patagónicos* (Patagonian smoked fish) such as *trucha* (trout) or *salmón*. And perhaps some *paté* or *salamín de ciervo* (venison) and *salame* or *bondeola de jabalí* (wild boar salami or cured pork shoulder similar to Italian capicola).

Interlaced among the meat is a bounty of *queso*—smoked, cubed, rolled, uncut and sliced *reggianito*, *romanito*, fontina, sardo, Camembert or brie and Roquefort. Edam, gruyère and gouda are also popular. The one that you are most likely to find is *queso pategrás*, a semi-hard yellow cheese of Argentine origin.

The *picada* always includes proper bread with a good crust, such as sliced baguette, along with olives in brine, *morrones asados en aceite de oliva* (roasted red peppers marinated in olive oil), *berenjena al escabeche* (pickled eggplant), *papas fritas* (potato chips) and *maní* (peanuts), to name a few possibilities. More filling options, such as *empanadas*, *tortillas* and *albóndigas* (meatballs), may be served as well.

While it's not traditional for dulce de leche to make an appearance at this savory spread, I've included some of my favorite gently sweetened finger foods here. A judicious amount of dulce de leche makes every one of these cocktail-hour snacks a little bit more special.

BACON-WRAPPED JALAPEÑOS

I haven't met many people who can resist this spicy, sweet and savory take on the classic happy-hour stuffed jalapeño oozing a deliciously creamy filling. Bacon, as it so often does, provides the salty, porky crunch that elevates these simple snacks, and dulce de leche gives the cream cheese a subtle complexity.

12 jalapeño peppers

8 ounces cream cheese, room temperature

½ cup traditional dulce de leche

1 clove garlic, chopped

¼ teaspoon smoked paprika

Pinch of salt

12 slices uncured bacon, cut in half

SPECIAL EQUIPMENT

24 toothpicks

Preheat the oven to 400°F. Line a large rimmed baking sheet with parchment or aluminum foil and fit a wire rack on top.

Cut the jalapeños in half lengthwise and remove seeds and ribs.

In a bowl, mix together the cream cheese, dulce de leche, garlic and paprika until well combined. Add a pinch of salt to taste. Spoon the filling mixture equally into the jalapeño halves.

Wrap each stuffed jalapeño half with a piece of bacon and secure with a toothpick. (The peppers can be prepared up to this point 1 day ahead and refrigerated, covered with plastic wrap.)

Transfer the jalapeños , stuffing side up, to the rack and bake for 25 to 28 minutes, or until the bacon is crisp to your liking. For extra crispy bacon, turn the oven to broil for the last minute or two. Serve immediately. Any leftovers keep, covered in plastic wrap, in the refrigerator for up to 4 days. Reheat before eating.

MANCHEGO FONDUE

A potful of melted cheese remains a perfect cocktail party food. Manchego, produced in the La Mancha region of Spain (home to Don Quixote), is a firm cheese made from unpasteurized sheep's milk; its nutty flavor varies in intensity depending on how long it has aged. Although crumbly and dry, Manchego melts velvety smooth. It pairs splendidly with dulce de leche, striking just the right balance between savory and sweet.

2 tablespoons cornstarch

1¼ pounds Manchego cheese, shredded

Pinch of salt

1 garlic clove, peeled

1 cup dry white wine

1 tablespoon lemon juice

⅓ cup traditional dulce de leche

¼ teaspoon cracked black pepper

¼ teaspoon grated nutmeg

ACCOMPANIMENTS FOR DIPPING
Crusty bread, cut into bite-size pieces; chorizo, cut into small pieces; green apple chunks; baby portobello mushrooms; broccoli florets

SPECIAL EQUIPMENT
Fondue pot and fondue forks or wooden skewers

Put the cornstarch in a small bowl. Add the cheese and salt, and toss to coat.

Rub the inside of a fondue pot with the garlic clove, then discard garlic. Add the wine and lemon juice to the pot and bring to a gentle simmer over medium heat, stirring constantly. Add the dulce de leche and stir until melted and thoroughly incorporated. Gradually stir in the coated cheese (melting the cheese gradually encourages a smooth fondue).

Season with the pepper and nutmeg. Reduce the heat to medium-low to maintain the temperature and serve with an assortment of small foods for dipping.

PANQUEUES

with Torta del Casar

Every time Gastón makes *panqueques,* he doubles or triples the recipe so that we'll have them in the refrigerator to enjoy throughout the week—at breakfast, tea time, dinner, dessert and occasionally for *picadas* too.

Torta del Casar—a Spanish cheese made from raw sheep's milk in the Extremadura region near the Portuguese border—has the perfect consistency for spreading on a paper-thin *panqueque.* Named after Casar de Cáceres, its city of origin, the shepherds who made the cheese used to call it *atortao* because it was shaped like a cake or *torta.* With a strong mature taste, Torta del Casar is slightly salty and bitter. It is so soft it can be eaten with a spoon. In fact, many cheesemongers prefer to sell only whole wheels because traditionally, one cuts the top off and dips bread into the runny cheese encased in the rind. I often buy it in a spread version, as the whole wheel can harden after you cut into it.

Feel free to substitute any soft, spreadable white cheese, such as double- or triple-cream brie or a soft cheese from your local producer. I even roll these *panqueques* up with country ham, and they're just divine.

3 large eggs

2 cups milk

1 cup all-purpose flour, preferably unbleached

¼ teaspoon salt

4 tablespoons butter, melted, plus more for coating the pan

2 tablespoons granulated sugar

1 (2 x 5.3 ounce/150 gram) package Torta del Casar cheese spread or a wheel of Torta del Casar

2 cups traditional dulce de leche

Put the eggs, milk, flour, salt, melted butter and sugar in a blender and blend for 30 seconds, or until smooth. Scrape down the mixture from the side of the blender and repeat, if necessary. Cover and refrigerate for at least 1 hour (2 hours is preferable), or up to 24 hours.

If the chilled batter has separated, gently stir it until it comes back together. Lightly butter a 6- or 7-inch nonstick pan and heat over medium-high heat until hot. Lift the pan from the heat and pour in 2 to 3 tablespoons of batter, tilting and rotating the pan to coat the surface. Return the pan to the heat and cook the *panqueque* until almost dry on top and lightly browned on the edges, about 1 minute. Loosen the edges and, using your fingers or a spatula, flip and cook the other side for about 15 seconds or until lightly browned. Make more with the remaining batter in the same manner, coating the pan with butter (we peel back the paper on the stick of butter and wipe it on the pan), as

CONTINUED

needed, and stacking the *panqueques* after they are cooked. They may be kept, wrapped in plastic wrap and refrigerated, for up to 3 days.

Place a *panqueque* on a work surface and carefully spread some Torta del Casar over the warm center. With a spatula, generously spread dulce de leche over the cheese. Fold the *panqueque* in half, then fold in half again, forming a triangle that is 4 layers thick. Prepare more in the same manner and fan them out on a platter. Serve immediately.

GRILLED NECTARINES

This is a pleasing fruit dish that we often serve as an appetizer at our regular Sunday afternoon *asado*. In Argentina, a light *picada* is always served as a meal opener to the *asado*. Just make sure there is plenty of bread to soak up the velvety cream left on the plate after the hot grilled nectarines have married the cloud-like ricotta and velvety dulce de leche.

6 ripe white nectarines

2 teaspoons olive oil

1½ cups traditional dulce de leche

1½ cups ricotta cheese

Fresh mint leaves, for garnish

Preheat a grill to medium high. When the grill is ready, halve and pit the nectarines, then lightly brush the cut sides with the olive oil. Grill the nectarines flesh sides down, without moving them, for about 5 minutes or until pronounced char lines have formed.

On each of 6 plates, spread ¼ cup dulce de leche, and then spoon ¼ cup of ricotta on top. Place two nectarine halves, grilled side up, on top of the ricotta and garnish with fresh mint leaves.

VARIATION: If peaches are more readily available, you can substitute them for the nectarines.

The Wisdom of Dorita

AS A NEWLY MINTED college graduate, my parents invited me on a cruise through the Canal de Panamá as Dorita's *acompañante* (date). One night we were on our own for dinner, and we opted to go to the casino instead and play the slot machines. Our money went quickly. On Dorita's last turn, three cherries lined up—one, two, three—on a diagonal. The lights flashed and a siren played, but not a single coin came out of the machine. "Well, *abuela*," I said, "I don't think you won." *"Claro,"* she answered. As we were leaving, a gentleman caught up with Dorita and handed her a claim ticket for the $500 she had indeed won on her machine. And with that we went to the casino bar for a celebratory *picada*.

As we sat enjoying our draft beer and *fiambres* (cold cuts), *quesos, aceitunas* (olives) and *maní* (peanuts), Dorita talked of her mother's Sunday evening ritual of artfully preparing a *picada* that consisted of the week's *restos* (leftovers) for the family to share. Josefina was clever about reinventing the food into bite-sized snacks: from rustic *chorizos* (sausages) served at the previous day's *asado,* to *milanesitas* (breaded and pounded meat), to *palmitos* with *salsa golf* (hearts of palm topped with a blend of ketchup and mayonnaise), to *bocaditos de tortilla* (small pieces of fried-potato omlet) that she would top with cheese and marinated olives. As they ate, Josefina told them long-winded stories of Dorita's grandmother who grew up in Olite, a provincial town in the Basque province of Navarra in Spain. Dorita reminded me, *"No te olvides de donde venis, Jose"* ("Never forget where you come from, Josie").

MORTADELLA CANAPÉS

I wasn't introduced to mortadella, the Italian cured sausage resembling bologna in size and taste, until I visited southern Argentina. We were sharing a *picada* of *ahumados patagónicos* (smoked cold cuts from the Patagonia) and the waiter explained that the mortadella is made of local *jabalí* (wild boar) that is first ground and then mashed into a paste. In Argentina, mortadella is often spiced with peppercorns and may also contain *piñones* (pine nuts); it is always served very thinly sliced. This make-ahead canapé pairs the taste of pork with the sweetness of dulce de leche and earthy pumpernickel bread. The dark stacks of cocktail bread slathered with dulce de leche butter create an eye-catching layered base.

1½ tablespoons unsalted butter, softened

1½ tablespoons traditional dulce de leche

12 (3-inch square) slices cocktail pumpernickel bread

12 slices mortadella (about ¼ pound), thinly sliced

In a small bowl, mix together the butter and dulce de leche, stirring until combined well. Spread 1 teaspoon of the butter mixture on 1 slice of bread. Top with another slice of bread and spread with another teaspoon of the butter mixture. Continue to layer 4 additional slices in the same manner, but do not butter the top slice. Make another bread stack by layering and buttering the remaining 6 bread slices in the same manner. Transfer the two prepared bread stacks to a plate and refrigerate, covered with plastic wrap, for 1 hour.

Just before serving, cut each bread stack vertically into 6 thin slices using a very sharp knife. Arrange the slices horizontally on a serving platter and top each with a slice of mortadella.

QUESO FRESCO & BACON PANINI

After having our fourth boy, Ignacio (Nacho), Gastón and I decided that we had to re-evaluate the way we managed weeknight dinner. We'd both come home exhausted from work and needed an easy solution. And that's how Thursday panini nights came to be. I like to use *queso fresco* as it is readily available in supermarkets, has a light mild taste and melts well. This Mexican cheese is traditionally made from raw cow's milk or a combination of cow's and goat's milk. In the States, you'll most likely find pasteurized versions. (*Queso fresco* is not to be confused with *queso blanco*, a similar-looking mild Mexican cheese that doesn't melt and is best used for frying or grilling.)

1 (12-ounce) package uncured smoked bacon

1 large ciabatta loaf

2 teaspoons extra-virgin olive oil

⅓ cup traditional dulce de leche

9 ounces queso fresco

2 cups baby arugula

SPECIAL EQUIPMENT
A panini press

Preheat the oven to 350°F. Preheat a panini press to high or heat a heavy skillet. Arrange the strips of bacon on an aluminum foil-lined baking sheet and bake until crisp, about 20 minutes. Transfer the bacon to paper towels to drain.

Cut the ciabatta in half lengthwise. Thinly brush each half with 1 teaspoon of the olive oil. Spread the dulce de leche evenly on the bottom half, leaving a little bit of a border to prevent the dulce de leche from spilling out during the grilling.

Cut the *queso fresco* into even slices and spread over the dulce de leche, then layer with the crispy bacon and top with the arugula. Put the two halves of the bread together to form 1 large sandwich, then cut the sandwich in half on the diagonal. Put 1 half on the panini press, and close the top of the press gently. Grill the sandwich slowly and evenly until the filling is bubbling and the bread is slightly charred. Remove the sandwich and let cool slightly on a cutting board. Grill the other half of the sandwich in the same manner. When cool to the touch, cut each sandwich into 4 triangular shapes and enjoy while warm.

VARIATIONS: Fresh buffalo mozzarella, which also has a mild flavor and melts into strings of gooey goodness, is a delicious substitute for the *queso fresco*.

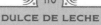

Two~Bite Mascarpone & Dulce de Leche Cannoli

Mini cannoli, stuffed with mascarpone and dulce de leche filling, are an ideal sweet finish to a casual *picada* or a fancy cocktail party. They look impressive, yet are quite easy to make. One to two days before your party, melt 6 ounces of bittersweet 60% chocolate chips in a double boiler and transfer to a small bowl, then melt 6 ounces of white melting wafers in the same manner. Dip 12 small hand-rolled cannoli shells in the dark chocolate, and another 12 shells in the white chocolate, transferring them to a wire cooling rack for a few hours, or until the chocolate sets. You can store these, lightly covered, in a cool place for up to 2 days.

When you are ready to fill the cannoli, mix 8 ounces of mascarpone with 4 ounces confectionary dulce de leche until blended and refrigerate for 30 minutes. Using a pastry bag, pipe the mixture into the prepared cannoli shells. These are best served fresh but may be kept up to 1 day in the refrigerator. Sprinkle the creamy filling with chopped pistachios or toasted coconut.

GOAT CHEESE SOUFFLÉS
WITH DULCE DE LECHE SAUCE

Mention the word *soufflé*, and even good cooks get nervous. The truth is these individual they are failproof once you premeasure the ingredients. A velvety white wine sauce is the perfect complement marrying earthy shallots and thyme with the subtle sweetness of dulce de leche. While this makes a great *picada*, it is also a festive side dish with poultry or pork.

FOR THE SOUFFLÉS

3½ tablespoons unsalted butter

⅓ cup all-purpose flour

1⅓ cups whole milk

4 large eggs, separated

2 teaspoons Dijon mustard

1 teaspoon finely chopped fresh thyme leaves

8 ounces goat cheese, crumbled, divided

Salt and freshly ground pepper, to taste

FOR THE SAUCE

1 teaspoon olive oil

1 shallot, finely diced

1 teaspoon finely chopped fresh thyme leaves

1 cup dry white wine

¾ cup heavy cream

2 heaping tablespoons traditional dulce de leche

Crusty bread, as an accompaniment

PREPARE THE SOUFFLÉS: Preheat the oven to 375°F. Butter six ¾-cup ramekins (3¾-by-2-inches). Boil enough water for a hot-water bath.

In a saucepan over low heat, melt the butter. Add the flour and cook the roux, whisking, for 3 minutes. Whisk in the milk. Increase the heat to medium and bring to a boil, whisking constantly, then reduce the heat and simmer, whisking occasionally, for 3 minutes more.

Remove the pan from the heat and add the egg yolks, mustard, thyme, two-thirds of the cheese and salt and pepper to taste, whisking until the cheese is melted. Transfer the yolk mixture to a large bowl.

In a large bowl, beat the egg whites with a pinch of salt on high speed with an electric mixer until they just hold soft peaks. Stir a quarter of the egg whites into the yolk mixture to lighten, then gently fold in the remaining egg whites and cheese until well combined. Divide the soufflé mixture among the ramekins and place them in a large deep pan; carefully add enough boiling water to the pan to reach about halfway up the sides of the ramekins. Bake the soufflés until puffed and golden brown, about 25 to 30 minutes.

PREPARE THE CREAM SAUCE: In a saucepan, heat the olive oil over medium heat, then add the shallot and thyme and cook, stirring constantly, until the shallot is translucent, 3 to 5 minutes. Add the wine and bring to a boil. Reduce the heat to medium-low and continue to boil for 5 minutes, stirring occasionally.

Strain through a fine-mesh sieve into a bowl, discarding the solids, and return the liquid to the saucepan over medium-low heat. Stir in the cream and the dulce de leche until combined well. Slowly bring the sauce to a boil, stirring occasionally, then reduce the heat and simmer for 1 minute.

When the soufflés are ready, remove from the oven and place on a large wooden board alongside crusty bread. Spoon 2 tablespoons of the cream sauce over each soufflé and serve immediately.

GRILLED PEACH PIZZAS

WITH MASCARPONE

Pizza for dessert is the perfect way to end a *picada*, especially if the grill is already heated up for another dish. This is the same dough that we use to make savory pizzas on the grill and the result is a crisp, chewy crust with great smoky flavor.

FOR THE DOUGH

1 ounce fresh yeast or ¾ ounce active dried yeast (3 [¼-ounce] packages)

2 generous tablespoons raw honey

8 cups unbleached bread flour

2 tablespoons sea salt

FOR THE TOPPING

4 fresh peaches, cut in half, pitted, then cut in half again, for a total of 16 slices

6 heaping tablespoons traditional or confectionary dulce de leche

6 heaping tablespoons mascarpone cheese

Large handful fresh mint leaves

MAKE THE DOUGH: In a small bowl, stir together the yeast, raw honey and 1 cup of tepid water until combined well. Let stand until the yeast is completely dissolved and the mixture bubbles, about 5 minutes.

On a clean surface, combine the bread flour and sea salt and arrange it in a mound. (Or combine them in a large bowl.) Make a well in the center and pour in the yeast mixture. Mix together with your hands until all the yeasty liquid is soaked up, and then add enough tepid water (up to 3 cups more), as needed, to gradually incorporate all the flour and to form a moist dough.

If working in a bowl, turn out the dough onto a work surface. With floured hands, knead the dough for 5 minutes.

Cut the dough in half and form into two rounds. Place on a baking sheet and lightly flour the top of each round. Score tops deeply with a knife, and let the dough rise in a dark, warm place for at least 1 hour.

When the dough has doubled in size, punch each round down to form a ball. Place one of the in a freezer-safe bag and freeze to use at a later time. The other dough round can be used immediately or wrapped in plastic and stored in the refrigerator for up to 1 day, or frozen for 2 weeks. Bring the dough to room temperature before proceeding with the recipe.

ROLL OUT THE DOUGH: Dust a large baking sheet with flour. Just before you are ready to grill, divide each round into two pieces. Working with 1 piece at a time, roll out the dough into an irregular thin round shape no more than ¼ inch thick. With your hands make a generous crust to hold the toppings and place the round on the baking sheet. Roll out the other piece of dough in the same manner and stack on top of the first round with a sheet of waxed paper or parchment paper between them.

PREPARE THE GRILL FOR HIGH HEAT AND MAKE THE TOPPING: When the coals are hot, grill the peach over direct heat about 5 minutes on each side to create grill mark.

Meanwhile, in a bowl, mix together the dulce de leche and the mascarpone cheese with a spatula until creamy. Set aside.

GRILL THE PIZZAS: Place the dough rounds, crust-sides down, on the grill and grill just long enough to firm up the crusts so they can be flipped over easily, about 3 minutes. With the aid of a large metal spatula, flip over the rounds. Immediately spread a generous layer of the cheese mixture over the rounds, leaving a 1-inch border from the crust, then arrange the grilled peaches on top. Cover the grill and cook the pizzas for about 5 minutes more. Using the metal spatula, remove the pizzas to a cutting board and sprinkle with the fresh mint. Cool for a few minutes to set the toppings, then cut into wedges for serving.

BURRATA CAPRESE SALAD

Gastón and I have a thing about burrata, the fresh mozzarella filled with cream and curds. Its rich interior surprises every time. I make this salad year-round—throughout the summer with heirloom tomatoes, in the colder months with roasted Campari tomatoes. If you can't find burrata, fresh whole-milk buffalo mozzarella can be substituted.

FOR THE DRESSING

½ cup olive oil

¼ cup white balsamic vinegar

½ cup or a handful of julienned fresh basil leaves

½ teaspoon shallot, grated on a microplane

1 teaspoon Dijon mustard

1 tablespoon traditional dulce de leche

Sea salt

Freshly ground black pepper

FOR A WINTER SALAD

2 pounds Campari tomatoes or organic cherry tomatoes

¼ cup olive oil

18 whole basil leaves

Salt and freshly ground pepper, to taste

FOR A SUMMER SALAD

6 ripe heirloom tomatoes

3 (2.5-ounce) rounds burrata cheese or 1 pound buffalo mozzarella, cut into quarters

18 whole basil leaves

Crusty bread, as an accompaniment

MAKE THE DRESSING: Put the olive oil, vinegar, basil leaves, shallot, mustard, traditional dulce de leche, sea salt and freshly ground pepper in a jar and shake for 30 seconds. Make sure the dulce de leche is completely incorporated. Set aside.

FOR THE WINTER SALAD: Preheat the oven to 200°F. In a medium bowl, toss the Campari tomatoes with the olive oil and season generously with salt and pepper. Place on a baking sheet. Bake for about 2 hours or until the tomatoes are softened. Remove from the oven and let cool on the baking sheet.

FOR THE SUMMER SALAD: Slice the heirloom tomatoes into ¼-inch-thick rounds.

TO SERVE (BOTH SALADS): Place two burrata quarters in the center of each of 6 plates, then fan the tomatoes and whole basil leaves around the cheese. Whisk the dressing to combine, then drizzle over the salad. Garnish with additional basil leaves and serve with bread.

RETRO BAKED BRIE

WITH PECANS

There are two good reasons baked brie became a cocktail-hour cliché back in the 1980s: First, it's completely delicious. Second, it looks impressive but takes about 5 minutes to assemble and just 20 minutes to bake, although it does need to cool for another 20 minutes before serving. I always enjoy watching guests dive into it with gusto. This winning combination suits almost any get-together, and I make it regularly as a holiday cocktail party appetizer. In summer, I skip the puff pastry and just serve slices of triple cream cheese topped with a bit of the dulce de leche mixture.

Much depends on the quality of your ingredients, as always, so make an effort to find the freshest pecans, or shell them yourself.

½ cup pecan halves, finely chopped

Grated zest of 1 large orange

½ cup confectionary dulce de leche

2 puff pastry sheets, thawed

1 16-ounce wheel brie or other triple cream cow's milk cheese

1 egg, beaten

Preheat the oven to 400°F. In a medium bowl, mix together the pecans, orange zest and dulce de leche. Spread on top of the brie.

Unfold the pastry on a floured surface. Carefully invert the wheel of brie and place it in the center of the pastry, topping side down. Fold the edges of the pastry over the cheese to cover. Trim excess pastry and press to seal. Reserve scraps or use the second sheet for decoration, if desired.

Brush the bottom seam of the pastry with the beaten egg. Place the cheese with pastry seam-side down on a baking sheet lined with parchment. Decorate the top with pastry cut-outs, if desired, and brush with the beaten egg. Bake for 25 minutes or until golden brown. Let the baked brie cool for 20 minutes before serving with crackers and sliced apples.

En la
Cena

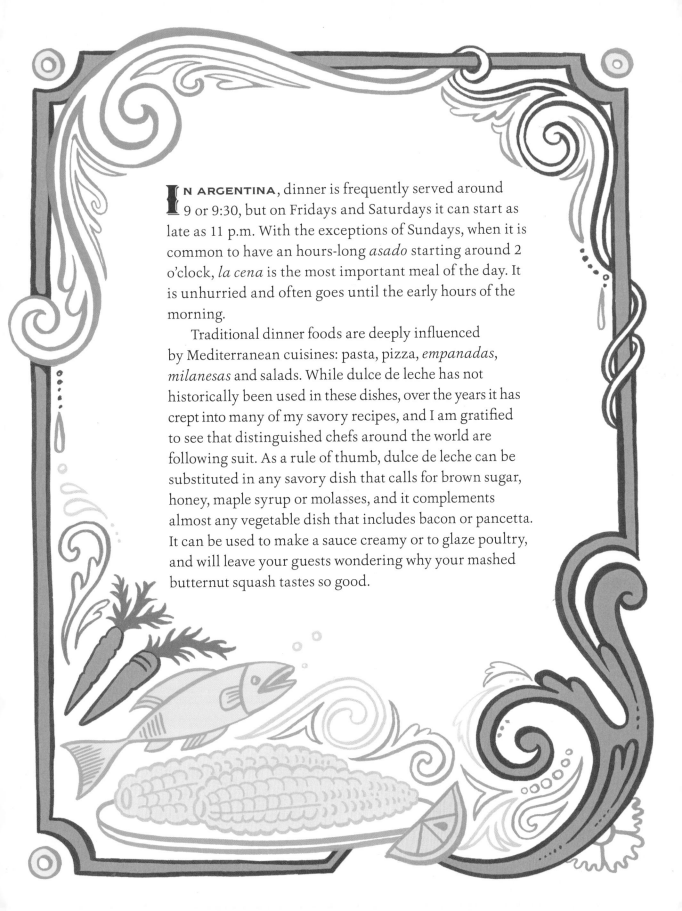

IN ARGENTINA, dinner is frequently served around 9 or 9:30, but on Fridays and Saturdays it can start as late as 11 p.m. With the exceptions of Sundays, when it is common to have an hours-long *asado* starting around 2 o'clock, *la cena* is the most important meal of the day. It is unhurried and often goes until the early hours of the morning.

Traditional dinner foods are deeply influenced by Mediterranean cuisines: pasta, pizza, *empanadas*, *milanesas* and salads. While dulce de leche has not historically been used in these dishes, over the years it has crept into many of my savory recipes, and I am gratified to see that distinguished chefs around the world are following suit. As a rule of thumb, dulce de leche can be substituted in any savory dish that calls for brown sugar, honey, maple syrup or molasses, and it complements almost any vegetable dish that includes bacon or pancetta. It can be used to make a sauce creamy or to glaze poultry, and will leave your guests wondering why your mashed butternut squash tastes so good.

FIGS IN PROSCIUTTO

This taste of summer is a happy dinner party starter and is super easy to make on a whim. Its beauty lies in simplicity and freshness: rustic prosciutto or country ham wrapped around succulent figs with a dulce de leche drizzle. I often serve these on a bed of butter lettuce or baby arugula as a starter.

12 whole black mission figs

12 slices prosciutto, about ¼ pound

¼ cup traditional dulce de leche

12 fresh mint leaves, chopped, for garnish

SPECIAL EQUIPMENT
Round toothpicks

If the figs are large, cut them in half; if they are small, keep whole.

Cut the slices of prosciutto in half. Wrap each fig or fig half with the prosciutto and secure with a toothpick. Depending on the size of the figs, you may have some leftover prosciutto. Drizzle dulce de leche over the figs. Garnish with the mint.

SERVES 6

SWEET POTATO RAVIOLI

with Sage Brown Butter

Many years ago I learned the trick of substituting wonton wrappers for fresh pasta sheets, and I've been making ravioli this way ever since. As a young girl, I often "helped" Dorita make fresh pastas like ravioli and *ñoqui*. She would lightly flour the tops of her kitchen stools to prepare little work surfaces for my sisters and me. Dorita would prepare and cut the pasta sheets on the *mesada* (counter), dollop teaspoons of the filling along half of the sheets and pass them down to us to assemble and seal. I now rely on my boys to do the same. This sage brown butter sauce is so simple yet extremely tasty.

FOR THE FILLING

1 large sweet potato, peeled and cubed

¼ cup finely grated Parmesan cheese

2 tablespoons ricotta

3 tablespoons traditional dulce de leche

Pinch of salt, or to taste

Pinch of freshly ground black pepper, or to taste

Pinch of freshly grated nutmeg, or to taste

FOR THE RAVIOLI

1 (12-ounce) package all-natural wonton wrappers

1 large egg

2 tablespoons olive oil

MAKE THE FILLING: Put the sweet potato pieces in a saucepan fitted with a steamer basket and steam for 20 minutes or until cooked through. Transfer to a bowl and mash until smooth. Stir in the Parmesan, ricotta and dulce de leche until combined and season with salt, pepper and nutmeg to taste. Let the filling cool for 10 minutes.

MAKE THE RAVIOLI: Lightly flour a baking sheet. Arrange half of the wonton wrappers on a cutting board, reserving the rest. In a small bowl, beat together the egg with 1 tablespoon water to form an egg wash. Brush the wonton wrappers with the egg wash. Spoon 1 tablespoon sweet potato filling onto the center of each wrapper and top each with a reserved wrapper. Using your fingers, seal the edges around the filling, pushing out the air.

Place the ravioli on the baking sheet and cover with a clean towel. (If you find you have too many ravioli, you can freeze them uncooked: Line a freezer-grade plastic storage container with wax paper and arrange ravioli in single layers with wax paper between each layer. To cook the ravioli from frozen, toss them into gently boiling salted and oiled water and cook 3 minutes.)

MAKE THE SAUCE: In a large saucepan, melt the butter over medium

CONTINUED

FOR THE SAGE BROWN BUTTER

½ cup (1 stick) unsalted butter, cut into pieces

6 large fresh sage leaves or ¼ cup fresh basil leaves, torn into pieces or thinly sliced

½ teaspoon salt, or to taste

¼ teaspoon freshly ground black pepper, or to taste

Grated Parmesan cheese

heat until it takes on a pale golden sheen, about 5 minutes. Add the sage leaves and cook until crisp, about 2 minutes. Stir in the salt and pepper. Keep the sauce warm over low heat.

COOK THE RAVIOLI: Bring a large pot of salted water to a gentle boil. Add the olive oil. Working in small batches to prevent the pasta from sticking together, add the ravioli to the boiling water and cook until tender, about 3 minutes. Using a slotted spoon, transfer the ravioli to a serving dish and cover to keep warm. Cook the remaining ravioli in the same manner.

To serve, spoon the sage brown butter over the ravioli and sprinkle with Parmesan cheese. Serve immediately.

DORITA APPROACHED EVERY MEAL as an opportunity to spoil her fellow diners. Some of her favorite dishes included *milanesa de pollo y carne* (chicken and beef milanese), *tortilla de papa* (fried potato frittata), ravioli filled with butternut squash or sweet potatoes and *ñoqui de papa* (potato gnocchi).

True to her Argentine heritage, Dorita faithfully prepared *ñoqui* on the 29th of each month. On this day, tradition dictates that you eat the *ñoqui* with money under your plate to ensure good luck and prosperity.

As a child, one of my favorite jobs was flicking the *ñoqui* off the tines of a fork to give them their characteristic shape. You could always tell the ones Dorita had prepared, as unlike mine, her dumplings were perfectly ridged on one side with a scooped indentation on the other. Still, she never minded. She would mix my messy *ñoqui* among the rest, knowing I would delight in eating them.

Dorita served them with different seasonal sauces—in summer, brown butter with sage or fresh marinara; in cooler weather, a rich dulce de leche white wine cream sauce with julienned ham and walnuts. She would pull out her little money satchel and slide a *peso* under each of our plates while we impatiently awaited her simple blessing—"*¡Buen provecho!*" ("Enjoy your meal!")—and then we would all dig in.

ROASTED GARLIC & DULCE DE LECHE SPREAD

It takes so little effort to roast a few heads of garlic, and the result is a great thing to cook with and eat. Roasted garlic offsets the sweetness of dulce de leche and enhances all of the flavors once they hit your palate. I always serve this with a loaf of rustic bread and often with a nice piece of ripe Camembert or other soft cheese as part of a casual dinner.

2 whole bulbs of garlic, unpeeled

1 teaspoon extra-virgin olive oil

2 sprigs fresh thyme

Salt, to taste

Freshly ground pepper, to taste

1 cup traditional dulce de leche

½ cup (1 stick) unsalted butter, softened

Crusty bread, as an accompaniment

Preheat the oven to 350°F. Place the garlic on a piece of heavy-duty aluminum foil, drizzle with the olive oil and top with the thyme. Season with salt and pepper and wrap the bulbs tightly in the foil. Place the bundle in a small bakingpan or on a small baking sheet and bake for about 1 hour. Let the garlic cool in the foil for about 5 minutes.

Open the foil and discard the thyme sprigs. Working with one bulb at a time over the bowl of a food processor, squeeze the garlic out of the skin, letting the garlic fall into the bowl. Pulse the cloves into a paste. Add the dulce de leche and the butter and process until smooth, scraping down the sides of the bowl as necessary. Transfer the garlic spread to a small bowl and refrigerate for 30 minutes to set.

CARROT SOUFFLÉ

Every Thanksgiving, without fail, my sister Barbara brings a carrot soufflé that we all love. The dish probably originated with two dear family friends, Marta and Blima. My version uses dulce de leche instead of sugar, which makes it a bit less sweet. This soufflé is an impressive and nourishing side for any poultry or pork dish.

FOR THE SOUFFLÉ

1 pound carrots, peeled and chopped into 1-inch pieces

3 large eggs

1 cup traditional dulce de leche

3 tablespoons all-purpose flour

2 teaspoons baking powder

½ cup (1 stick) unsalted butter, melted

1 dash ground cinnamon

¼ teaspoon salt

FOR THE TOPPING

¼ cup corn flake crumbs

¼ cup chopped walnuts

3 tablespoons light brown sugar

2 tablespoons unsalted butter, melted

MAKE THE SOUFFLÉ: Preheat the oven to 350°F. Lightly butter a 13-by-9-by-2-inch casserole dish. In a saucepan, cook in boiling salted water until very soft, about 7 minutes. Dry transfer the carrots to the bowl of a food processor and let cool for 5 minutes.

Process the carrots until smooth, then add the eggs, dulce de leche, flour, baking powder, melted butter, cinnamon and salt and pulse until well combined. Pour into the casserole, smoothing the top.

MAKE THE TOPPING: Add the corn flake crumbs, walnuts, light brown sugar and melted butter to the cleaned bowl of the food processor and pulse just until a crumble is formed. Spread evenly over the top.

Bake the soufflé for 40 minutes or until puffy and lightly browned. Serve immediately.

ORANGE CAULIFLOWER

with Dulce de Leche & Cumin

 range cauliflower comes into peak season during the fall months, and it is slightly sweeter and creamier than the common white variety. The extra beta carotene accounts for a striking color, and it contains more vitamin A. Roasting creates a nutty tenderness, while dulce de leche spiked with cumin and lime adds a burst of flavor.

1 orange cauliflower head

½ cup traditional dulce de leche

1 lime, zested and juiced

¼ teaspoon ground cumin

Sea salt

Freshly ground black pepper

Small handful flat-leaf parsley, chopped

Preheat the oven to 400°F. Lightly oil a small baking sheet. Trim the base of the cauliflower to remove any leaves and the woody stem.

In a medium bowl, combine the dulce de leche with the lime zest and juice, cumin, sea salt and pepper. Dunk the cauliflower head into the bowl and, with a brush or your hands, smear the mixture evenly all over its surface. (Any excess mixture can be refrigerated in an airtight container for up to 3 days and used with meat, fish or other vegetables.)

Place the cauliflower, stem side down, on the baking sheet and roast 30 to 40 minutes until the surface is dry and lightly browned. The dulce de leche mixture will form a crust. Let the cauliflower cool for 10 minutes, then sprinkle with the parsley before cutting it into wedges.

PORK CHOPS
WITH SAUTÉED APPLES

 huletas (pork chops) with sautéed apples is a common fall dish in Argentina and one of the first thing I cooked for Gastón when we were dating. Dorita used to say that you can win anyone over with your cooking just by sautéing onions or shallots with garlic—as long as you don't burn them. One of my mother-in-law's friends did just this as a newlywed. She would sauté the garlic and onions, then order take out. Her husband would walk in and be swayed by the aroma; he was convinced that she had worked for hours in the kitchen.

I like to add a bit of dulce de leche to the apples; it balances the flavor and keeps the pork moist, and I reserve some to top off each plate. Serve with basmati rice.

2 tablespoons olive oil, divided

6 (1-inch-thick) center cut bone-in pork loin chops

Sea salt

Freshly ground black pepper

3 shallots, finely chopped

1 clove garlic, finely chopped

2 sprigs fresh rosemary, chopped

3 apples, such as Gala or Granny Smith, peeled, cored and thinly sliced

1 cup dry white wine

1 cup low-sodium chicken broth

3 heaping tablespoons traditional dulce de leche

2 tablespoons unsalted butter

SPECIAL EQUIPMENT
An instant-read thermometer

Heat a skillet, preferably cast-iron, over medium-high heat, then add 1 tablespoon olive oil and swirl to coat. Season the pork chops with sea salt and pepper and add to the pan. Cook in the oil for 3 to 5 minutes on each side or until an instant-read thermometer inserted into a chop registers 145°F for medium doneness. Transfer chops to a warm platter and cover with foil to keep warm.

Add the remaining tablespoon olive oil, shallots, garlic and rosemary to the skillet, season with sea salt and pepper, and cook, stirring constantly, until the shallots are soft and transparent, about 5 minutes. Add the apples and allow to brown. Add the wine, stirring to loosen any browned bits from the skillet, bring to a boil, and boil for about 3 minutes or until the wine is reduced by half. Reduce the heat to medium-low, then stir in the broth and dulce de leche and simmer until the apples are soft. Remove the pan from the heat and stir in the butter.

To serve, spoon the sautéed apples over the chops and drizzle with the remaining juices.

VARIATION: This dish is equally delicious with sautéed peaches. Substitute 3 peaches, each cut into 8 wedges, for the apples.

SERVES 6

MOM'S POLYNESIAN CHICKEN

As a child, I would often wake in the morning to find my mother preparing dinner and breakfast simultaneously. She worked with my father at his medical office, but she always made sure we sat down as a family for dinner. This was one of her favorite quick stir-fries and has become one I also turn to when time is tight. Dulce de leche adds a smooth finish to the tangy sweet-and-sour sauce.

¼ cup olive oil, divided

2 shallots, diced

2 jalapeño peppers, seeded and finely diced

½ teaspoon salt

1 red bell pepper, diced

4 skinless boneless chicken breasts (about 1.3 pounds), cut into 1-inch cubes

1 cup fresh pineapple in 1-inch chunks

½ cup traditional dulce de leche

¼ teaspoon cayenne pepper

Large handful of fresh cilantro, chopped

Basmati rice, for serving

In a large skillet, heat 2 tablespoons of the olive oil over medium heat until hot but not smoking, then add the shallots, jalapeño peppers and salt and cook, stirring, until the shallots soften and become translucent, about 5 minutes. Add the bell pepper and continue to cook, stirring constantly, until soft, about 5 minutes more. With a slotted spoon, transfer the vegetable mixture to a small bowl and set aside.

Add the remaining 2 tablespoons of olive oil to the skillet and heat over medium-high heat until hot but not smoking. Add the chicken cubes and cook, without stirring, for at least 5 minutes to brown, then continue to cook, stirring constantly, for 2 to 5 minutes more or until the cubes are brown on all sides.

Add the pineapple, dulce de leche, cayenne pepper and the reserved vegetable mixture and stir to combine. Cover the skillet and cook for 5 minutes more, or until the sauce boils and thickens. Remove the pan from the heat and stir in the cilantro. Serve warm with basmati rice.

SUPREMA DE POLLO MARYLAND

Unlikely as it seems, Chicken Maryland has become ingrained in Buenos Aires dining culture. In the United States, the name refers to a historic dish of fried chicken with gravy, but in Argentina and neighboring South American countries it has taken on a life of its own. (And throughout other food cultures, including Australia and Southeast Asia, it can refer to any number of variations on the chicken-dinner theme.)

The *suprema* is Argentina's beloved chicken *milanesa* that appears on every café menu. *Milanesa* may be served simply with lemon wedges or prepared *a la suiza* (the Swiss way), bathed in béchamel sauce and Parmesan cheese or *a la napolitana*, with tomato sauce, oregano and melted mozzarella.

In the Argentine version of *a la Maryland*, thinly pounded breast of chicken (often with the first wing joint still attached) is breaded, fried and served with creamed corn or peas, pancetta, roasted red peppers and a fried banana. Some cafés top it off with a fried egg. While the combination may seem odd, this sweet and salty dish is deeply delicious.

In fact, it was one of my *abuelo* Alfredo's favorites. We would often go to Café Tabac just around the corner from our apartment in Buenos Aires, and as the waiter approached our table, Alfredo would hold up two fingers and order, *"Dos supremas a la Maryland."* I've added my own twist by stuffing dulce de leche into the fried banana for a delightful contrast to the pancetta and roasted peppers. This dish has many moving parts, but it's not complicated. The challenge while eating it is to make sure each forkful consists of a little bit of everything.

FOR THE TOPPINGS

12 slices pancetta, about ¼ pound

Freshly ground black pepper, to taste

12 ounces roasted red peppers, for serving

Preheat the oven to 400°F. Line a baking sheet with aluminum foil. Arrange the pancetta slices on the sheet and season with pepper. Bake for 15 minutes or until desired crispness is achieved. Transfer to a paper towel-lined plate to drain. Set aside, covered with foil to keep warm.

MAKE THE BÉCHAMEL AND PEA SAUCE: In a medium saucepan, melt the butter over medium-low heat. Add the flour and stir until smooth. Increase the heat to medium and cook, stirring constantly, until the mixture turns light golden, 6 to 7 minutes.

CONTINUED

FOR THE BÉCHAMEL AND PEA SAUCE

5 tablespoons unsalted butter

4 tablespoons all-purpose flour

4 cups milk

2 cups frozen sweet peas, thawed

2 teaspoons salt

½ teaspoon freshly grated nutmeg

FOR THE CHICKEN MILANESE

6 boneless, skinless chicken breasts, about 2 pounds

3 large eggs

3 sprigs fresh thyme, finely chopped

¼ cup finely chopped fresh parsley

1 garlic clove, smashed and finely chopped

2 teaspoons lemon zest

½ teaspoon salt

¼ teaspoon freshly ground black pepper

About 3 cups unseasoned breadcrumbs

½ cup vegetable oil, for frying

FOR THE FRIED BANANAS

6 firm ripe bananas

4 tablespoons traditional dulce de leche, divided

2 large eggs

About 2 cups unseasoned breadcrumbs

½ cup vegetable oil, for frying

Meanwhile, heat the milk in another medium saucepan over moderately high heat until just about to boil.

Whisk the hot milk into the flour mixture, 1 cup at a time, whisking constantly until very smooth. Bring to a boil, then reduce the heat to medium-low and cook 7 minutes more, stirring constantly. Add the peas and cook for another 3 minutes. Remove from the heat. Season the béchamel with the salt and nutmeg, cover the pan and set aside.

PREPARE THE CHICKEN: Working with one piece of chicken at a time, place the breast on a cutting board. With the palm of one hand, press down, and using a sharp knife, carefully slice into the thickest part of the breast, drawing the knife almost all the way through. Open the breast and place the butterflied chicken between two sheets of heavy plastic wrap. Gently pound to an even ⅛-inch thickness with a meat mallet or rolling pin, being careful not to tear the meat. Butterfly and pound the remaining chicken in same manner.

In a shallow dish, beat the eggs with the thyme, parsley, garlic, lemon zest, salt and pepper. In another shallow dish, spread out the breadcrumbs. Working with one piece of chicken at a time, dip the chicken into the beaten egg mixture, coating it evenly, then press both sides into the breadcrumbs, coating it evenly. Gently toss the coated chicken between your hands to allow any excess crumbs to fall back into the dish, and transfer to a large plate. Coat the remaining chicken in the same manner, arranging the chicken without stacking.

PREPARE THE BANANAS: Working with one banana at a time, peel and carefully cut the banana in half lengthwise. Scoop out the seeds and fill each half with 1 teaspoon of dulce de leche. Reassemble the banana to sandwich the dulce de leche. Peel and fill the remaining bananas in the same manner. Beat the eggs in a shallow dish. Carefully dip 1 banana into the egg, then press into the breadcrumbs and transfer to a plate. Prepare the remaining bananas in the same manner.

FRY THE CHICKEN: Preheat the oven to 200°F. In a large skillet, heat the vegetable oil over medium heat and pan-fry the chicken, one piece at a time, about 2 to 4 minutes per side until golden brown and no longer pink in the middle. Transfer to a paper towel-lined plate to drain. Cover the plate loosely with foil and keep warm in the oven. Fry the remaining chicken in the same manner.

FRY THE BANANA: In a large skillet, heat the vegetable oil over medium heat and pan-fry the bananas, one at a time, about 2 to 4 minutes per side until golden brown. Transfer the cooked banana to a paper towel–lined plate to drain. Cover the plate loosely with foil and keep warm in the oven with the chicken. Fry the remaining bananas in the same manner.

To serve, place 1 chicken milanese on each plate and top with a fried banana. Spoon some béchamel and pea sauce on the side and top with two slices of the pancetta and roasted pepper.

ORANGE-GLAZED ROAST TURKEY

I was in my early twenties when I spent my first Thanksgiving away from home. I had just moved back to Buenos Aires and met Gastón. To my surprise, on Thanksgiving Day, he asked if I'd like to have dinner with his family in La Plata. Their table was filled with some of my Thanksgiving favorites—roasted *pavo* (turkey) with a *ciruela pasa* (prune) and sage stuffing and *puré mixto de calabaza y papa* (mashed potatoes mixed with butternut squash) and a spinach and walnut salad. My future father-in-law, Jorge Luis, had rubbed butter mixed with herbs and dulce de leche under the turkey's skin. The meat was delicate and moist, and the skin extra-crisp. As we lingered around the table for *sobremesa* (that moment after a meal when the conversation is still flowing), my future mother-in-law, Graciela, presented me with a *servilletero de cuernito* (a napkin holder made of antler). And with that simple gesture, the Orías let me know that I would always have a seat at their family table.

FOR THE ROSEMARY BUTTER

½ cup (1 stick) unsalted butter, softened

½ cup traditional dulce de leche

1 teaspoon finely chopped fresh rosemary leaves

Zest of 1 orange

FOR THE TURKEY

1 (13-pound) fresh turkey (reserve giblets for gravy)

Small bunch of fresh sage leaves

1 bulb garlic, broken into cloves and smashed

Salt and freshly ground black pepper

1 whole nutmeg for grating over the turkey

MAKE THE ROSEMARY BUTTER: In a small bowl stir together the butter, dulce de leche, rosemary and orange zest. On a work surface, form the mixture into a log, wrap tightly in plastic wrap and refrigerate for at least 2 hours and up to 3 days or freeze for up to 2 weeks.

PREPARE AND ROAST THE TURKEY: Remove the giblets from the turkey (reserving for the gravy), then rinse the bird and pat dry. Place the turkey, breast up, on a rack in a large roasting pan. Using a spoon, carefully separate the skin from the breast to create room for the rosemary butter by starting at the side of the cavity just above the leg and carefully working up toward the breastbone and the back. With your hands, generously rub half the butter underneath the skin from front to back. Once the butter is rubbed in, layer the whole sage leaves evenly under the skin. (Don't be afraid to really get in there as it will create a self-basting moisture barrier while the turkey is roasting.) Rub the remaining rosemary butter all over the outside of the turkey and inside the cavity. Place sage leaves inside the cavity as well.

With a small knife, make 6 small slits in each thigh and drumstick and push a smashed garlic clove into each hole until it just peeps out. Liberally season the bird with salt, pepper and freshly grated nutmeg.

4 oranges, sliced into
 ¼-inch-thick rounds
3 oranges, juiced
3 cups dry white wine

SPECIAL EQUIPMENT
Toothpicks, an instant-read
thermometer

Tie the legs together with string and tuck the wing tips under the body. Cover the turkey with slices, using toothpicks to hold them in place to keep any loose skin around the cavity together. Place remaining orange slices inside the cavity.

Cover the turkey loosely with foil and allow to sit on the counter for 1 hour or keep in the refrigerator for up to 12 hours. (Take your turkey out of the refrigerator a few hours before roasting so it reaches room temperature.)

Preheat the oven to 350°F. Pour the orange juice and wine inside the cavity and in the pan. Keep the bird covered loosely with foil and roast for 3 to 3½ hours, or according to the weight of your turkey (generally, it takes 15 minutes per pound for a fresh turkey to reach 160°F on an instant-read thermometer inserted into the thickest part of the thigh). After the first hour of cooking, baste every 30 minutes. Remove the foil after 2 hours in order to brown the skin.

Transfer the turkey to a cutting board, keeping the juices in the pan to make the gravy (see page 154), and cover the bird with foil; let rest for 20 minutes before carving. Garnish the serving platter with more sliced oranges, if desired.

VARIATION: I often prepare a 6½-pound bone-in skin-on turkey breast instead of the whole bird. (A breast that size will feed 6 to 8 people.) Prepare following the directions above and roast it in a 350°F oven for about 1¾ hours. The breast will usually cook more quickly than the whole turkey, so start checking it after 1½ hours and continue roasting until a thermometer registers 160°F in the thickest part of the meat. Transfer to a cutting board and tent loosely with foil for 20 minutes. The temperature will continue to rise as it rests. Carve the breast and serve with Turkey Gravy (page 134).

TURKEY GRAVY

In Argentina it is common to eat every part of the animal, including the tripe, cow's stomach, liver, kidneys and gizzard. A typical weekday supper might consist of a plate of *menudos* (the liver, heart, gizzard and neck of a chicken or other fowl, usually removed before the bird is cooked and added to gravy, stuffing or soup) with white rice. While I'm not crazy about the taste on their own, I use the neck and giblets to make the stock for gravy.

1 bulb garlic

1¼ tablespoons olive oil, divided, plus more for drizzling

Salt

1 medium onion, finely chopped

2 celery stalks, finely chopped

1 medium carrot, finely chopped

Packet of neck and giblets from turkey, roughly chopped

4 cups low-sodium chicken broth

Half an orange

1 bay leaf

Pan juices from roasting the turkey

1 cup white wine

¼ cup all-purpose flour, plus additional if necessary

Freshly ground black pepper to taste

Preheat the oven to 350°F. Place the garlic on a piece of heavy-duty aluminum foil, drizzle with the olive oil and season with a pinch of salt. Wrap the garlic tightly in the foil. Place the bundle in a small ovenproof pan or baking sheet and bake for about 1 hour. Let the garlic cool in the foil for about 5 minutes.

Open the foil. Working over a small bowl, squeeze the cloves out of the skin, letting the garlic fall into the bowl. Mash the cloves into a paste.

In a large saucepan, heat 1 tablespoon of olive oil until hot but not smoking, then add the onion and a pinch of salt and cook over medium heat until translucent. Add the celery, carrot, neck and giblets and cook, stirring, until golden brown. Stir in the roasted garlic paste and chicken broth. Squeeze the juice from the orange half into the pan then add it and bay leaf. Bring the mixture to a boil, then reduce heat and simmer, covered, for 2½ hours.

Remove the bay leaf, neck and giblets from the stock, transfer the remaining mixture to a high-speed blender and blend until smooth. Strain the stock through a fine-mesh sieve into the cleaned saucepan.

Once the turkey is done, remove 2 cups of the juices from the roasting pan and stir into the stock. Add the wine and bring the mixture to a boil. Reduce the heat to medium-low and gradually add ¼ cup flour, whisking to combine. Continue to cook the mixture, whisking constantly and adding more flour, if necessary, for 3 to 5 minutes more until the gravy is thickened. Season with black pepper to taste.

PISTACHIO-CRUSTED SALMON

While Dorita was an amazing cook, she enjoyed a night off from the kitchen, especially here in the United States, when she often cooked for our family of eight. Our meals out went something like this: I would translate the entire menu for her, she'd ask me to repeat one or two dishes—and inevitably, she would opt for *salmón*. This is a simple meal you can prepare in less than thirty minutes. In the crust, crunchy pistachios contrast with sweet, tangy dulce de leche and lemon.

1 (3-pound) salmon fillet
   with skin

Juice of 1 lemon

4 tablespoons traditional
   dulce de leche

1 cup shelled pistachio nuts

½ cup panko breadcrumbs

2 tablespoons olive oil

½ teaspoon salt

½ teaspoon freshly ground
   pepper

Preheat the oven to 375°F. Put the salmon skin side down on a baking sheet lined with foil. In a small bowl, combine the lemon juice and dulce de leche, stirring until combined, then spread over the fish.

Put the pistachio nuts in a food processor and pulse until coarsely ground. Add the panko, olive oil, salt and pepper and pulse just to combine. Spread the pistachio mixture evenly over the dulce de leche mixture to cover the salmon.

Bake for 15 to 20 minutes or until the salmon is firm to the touch and has reached the desired doneness. (Test the thickest part of the fillet by carefully poking through with a fork. When the fish flakes easily, it's ready.) Remove the salmon from the oven, loosely cover with foil and let rest on the baking sheet for 5 to 10 minutes. Transfer to a serving platter and serve warm.

Calabaza

Argentina is the leading producer of *calabaza* (squash) in South America. Among the most popular variety of gourds is the *anquito* (butternut squash), which is commonly referred to as *calabaza*, even though there are many other indigenous varieties of squash that fall under the same general term. Butternut squash, with its hourglass shape, is a winter squash that is a staple in the cuisine. It appears in typical stews, such as *puchero* and *locro*; is used as a filling for savory *tartas* and pastas; and is commonly halved and stuffed with savory options, such as lentils, ground beef or corn, and roasted until golden.

Candied *zapallito* (pumpkin) or *calabazita en almíbar*—cubed firm squash with a crunchy exterior and pillowy interior that is preserved in sweet syrup—is a treat that can be eaten straight from the jar, served alongside a cheese tray at the *merienda* (tea time), or as a dessert course with fruit, nuts and cheeses. Something magical happens when you prepare squash and submerge it in a sweet liquid bath. The same can be said for roasted butternut squash when it's puréed with dulce de leche.

SERVES 6

BUTTERNUT SQUASH

WITH CRISPY SHALLOTS

In Argentina, mashed *calabaza* is just as common as mashed potatoes. In fact, many restaurants offer side-by-side purées of butternut squash and white potatoes. This dish pairs nicely with any type of poultry or *milanesa*.

2 medium butternut squash, peeled and cut into large cubes

3 tablespoons olive oil, divided, plus additional if necessary

1½ teaspoons salt

½ teaspoon freshly ground black pepper

3 shallots, peeled and sliced into thin rings

2 tablespoons unsalted butter, softened

2 tablespoons traditional dulce de leche

Preheat the oven to 400°F. Put the butternut squash on a baking sheet and toss with 1½ tablespoons of the olive oil and the salt and pepper, adding more oil as needed to coat lightly. Spread out the squash in a single layer and roast, turning once after about 20 minutes, for 40 minutes total or until tender.

Meanwhile, in a saucepan, heat the remaining 1½ tablespoons olive oil over medium-low heat until hot but not smoking, add the shallots, and cook, stirring infrequently to allow them to caramelize until brown and crisp, about 15 minutes. Remove from the heat and transfer the shallots to paper towels to drain.

When the squash is tender, transfer to a large mixing bowl. Add the butter and dulce de leche and blend with a handheld mixer until well combined. Serve hot, sprinkled with shallots.

SERVES 8

CARAMELIZED BRUSSELS SPROUTS

WITH PANCETTA

I f you're not yet convinced that dulce de leche isn't just for breakfast or dessert, this memorable side dish should persuade you. Dulce de leche contributes just the right amount of sweetness to the robust sprouts and salty pancetta.

1 teaspoon olive oil

4 ounces pancetta *cubetti* (little cubes) or finely chopped pancetta

1 large shallot, finely chopped

1½ pounds brussels sprouts, halved, or quartered if large

Pinch of salt

¼ cup traditional dulce de leche

Coat a very large skillet with the olive oil and heat the pan over medium heat until the oil is hot. Add the pancetta and shallot, and cook, stirring constantly, until the pancetta is crispy and the shallot is transparent, about 5 minutes. Using a slotted spoon, transfer the mixture to a small bowl and set aside.

Add the brussels sprouts to the pan, season with a pinch of salt and cook over high heat without stirring until browned, about 4 minutes. Reduce the heat to moderately low, add the dulce de leche and the reserved pancetta mixture and cook, stirring occasionally, until the dulce de leche forms a syrup and the sprouts are just crisp-tender, about 7 minutes more. Serve hot.

GLAZED CARROTS

When I make this dish, my boys (including Gastón) forget that they dislike cooked carrots. It's true comfort food, wholesome and satisfying. I use organic rainbow-colored carrots when I can.

2 pounds small carrots, peeled

¼ cup (½ stick) unsalted butter

¼ cup traditional dulce de leche

2 tablespoons lemon juice

Salt, to taste

Freshly ground black pepper, to taste

½ cup chopped flat-leaf parsley, for garnish

In a medium saucepan, cook the carrots in boiling salted water until just tender, 5 to 6 minutes. Drain and return to the pan. Add the butter, dulce de leche and lemon juice, cover the pan and bring just to a boil.

Reduce the heat to medium, uncover, and continue to cook the carrots, stirring occasionally, until glazed, about 10 minutes. Season with salt and pepper and garnish with the parsley.

139

EN LA CENA

GRILLED CORN
WITH DULCE DE LECHE CILANTRO BUTTER

Fresh corn on the cob is a hallmark of lazy summer evenings, and I often throw ears on the grill alongside the meat or fish. This sweet is a delicious and unique way to top the corn, so I keep a supply in the freezer. In fact, I triple the recipe whenever I make it so that there's always plenty for a quick side dish with other vegetables; I even toss it with hot popcorn on family movie nights.

½ cup (1 stick) unsalted butter, softened

½ cup traditional dulce de leche

½ teaspoon finely chopped fresh cilantro

Zest of 1 lime

6 ears yellow corn

In a small bowl, whisk together the butter, dulce de leche, cilantro and lime zest until combined well. On a work surface, form the mixture into a log, wrap tightly in plastic wrap and refrigerate for at least 2 hours and up to 3 days or freeze it for up to 2 weeks.

Preheat the grill to medium-high (350°F to 400°F). Pull back the husks from the corn, leaving them attached, and remove the silks. Pull the husks back over the corn and tie with kitchen string to form a handle. Fully submerge the corn in a bucket or sink filled with cold salted water for at least 10 minutes and up to 30 minutes, then drain.

Grill the corn, covered with the grill lid, for 15 minutes or until the husks are golden brown, turning occasionally with tongs. Pull back the husks, generously spread the butter over the hot corn and serve.

VARIATION: To prepare the corn indoors, husk and cook in a large saucepan of boiling salted water until crisp-tender, 7 to 10 minutes. Using tongs, transfer the corn to a platter and generously spread the butter mixture over the hot corn.

My Favorite Dulce de Leche Vinaigrette

Here's a delicious way to tame that kale salad. This vinaigrette originally came together one night for a simple sliced fennel, apple and arugula salad. I found that just a tablespoon of dulce de leche lends a creaminess to the standard acidic vinaigrette, cutting through the acidic tang of the vinegar. I add this dressing to greens, vegetables and soft cheeses, and even use it to marinate poultry or pork.

In a mason jar combine ½ cup olive oil, ¼ cup white balsamic vinegar, about ½ teaspoon grated shallot (1 small shallot grated on a microplane), ½ cup julienned fresh basil leaves, 1 tablespoon traditional dulce de leche, 1 teaspoon Dijon mustard, and sea salt and freshly ground black pepper to taste. Whisk to emulsify the dulce de leche and give the jar a good shake, then let the dressing rest for at least 10 minutes for the flavors to blend. The dressing keeps in the refrigerator for up to 5 days, but be sure to bring it to room temperature before using.

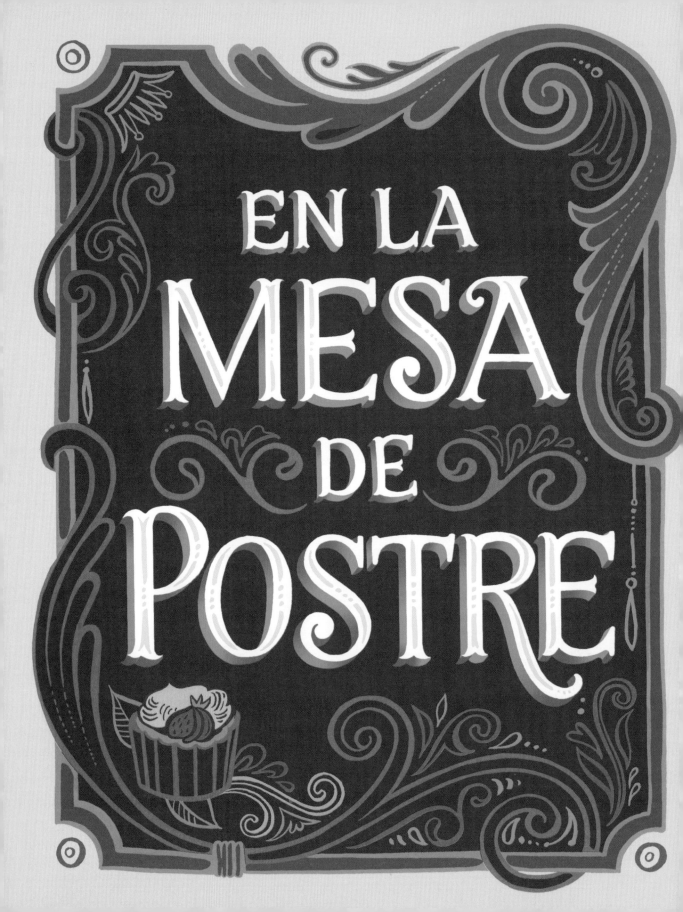

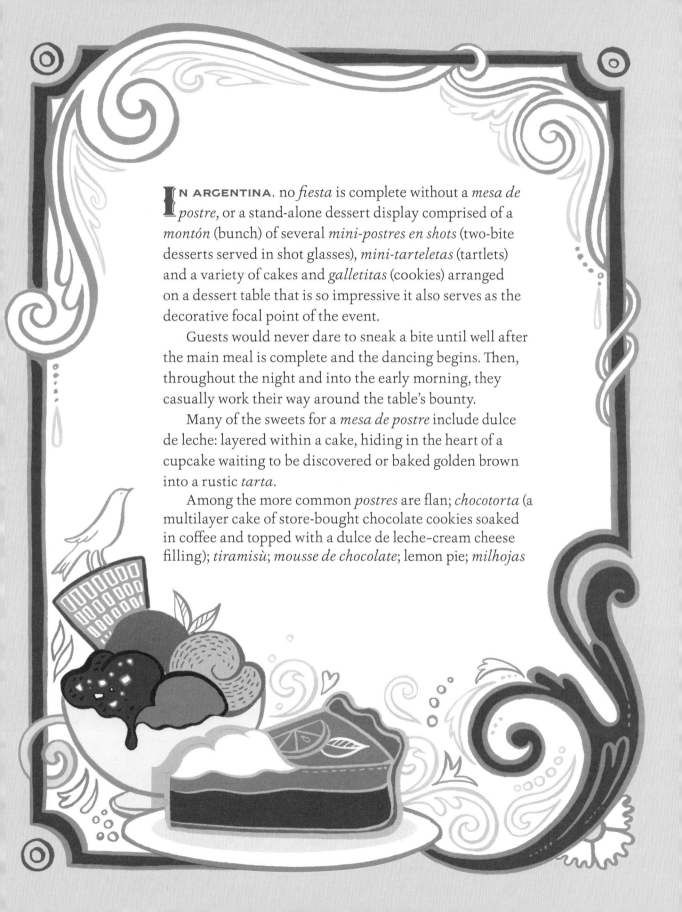

IN ARGENTINA, no *fiesta* is complete without a *mesa de postre*, or a stand-alone dessert display comprised of a *montón* (bunch) of several *mini-postres en shots* (two-bite desserts served in shot glasses), *mini-tarteletas* (tartlets) and a variety of cakes and *galletitas* (cookies) arranged on a dessert table that is so impressive it also serves as the decorative focal point of the event.

Guests would never dare to sneak a bite until well after the main meal is complete and the dancing begins. Then, throughout the night and into the early morning, they casually work their way around the table's bounty.

Many of the sweets for a *mesa de postre* include dulce de leche: layered within a cake, hiding in the heart of a cupcake waiting to be discovered or baked golden brown into a rustic *tarta*.

Among the more common *postres* are flan; *chocotorta* (a multilayer cake of store-bought chocolate cookies soaked in coffee and topped with a dulce de leche–cream cheese filling); *tiramisù*; *mousse de chocolate*; lemon pie; *milhojas* (the dulce-de-leche-packed Argentine version of a French napoleon); *tartas de manzana* (apple tartlets); and *pastafrola* (artisanal pie filled with dulce de leche or quince jam). Assorted tartlets with *frutas del bosque* (mixed berries) are also very popular, as are *panqueques rellenos de dulce de leche* (crêpes filled with dulce de leche) and *alfajores* (traditional Argentine sandwich cookies).

In *lo cotidiano* (everyday life), ice cream is a way of life. *Helado* is so popular that most every *barrio* has multiple *heladerías* that offer home delivery well past midnight. Dulce de leche is undoubtedly the most popular ice cream flavor in Argentina, and it comes in a variety of concoctions—*coco con dulce de leche* (with coconut), *granizado* (with chocolate bits), *brownies o mini Oreos*, *tramontana* (vanilla ice cream swirled with dulce de leche and bits of cookies bathed in dark chocolate) and last but not least, super *dulce de leche* (dulce de leche ice cream swirled with generous ribbons of more dulce de leche).

Dorita always liked to finish her day off with a bite-sized sweet note. *"La vida es muy corta."* ("Life is too short.") You have to treat yourself every now and then," she'd say, shrugging her shoulders. The following collection will give you a full range of dulce de leche desserts—from my most decadent carrot cake to an irresistible tiramisù to a simple ice cream, and everything else in between.

DIVINE CARROT LAYER CAKE

Dorita was known for her *torta de nuez* (nut cake), and I've come into my own bit of fame since I started making this cake with three thick layers of dulce de leche. In fact, years ago when I couldn't find dulce de leche in our local market, this is the cake that led me to finally make my own.

I've had people ask me if I use food coloring to achieve the candy-orange color, but it really is only due to the quantity of carrots in the batter. Be sure to use a food processor to shred them quickly. This is an impressive cake for a special party. For a simpler two-layer version, cut the recipe in half. The cake is superb by itself, but that much sweeter with cream cheese frosting.

FOR THE CAKE

4 cups all-purpose flour

4 cups granulated sugar

2 teaspoons baking powder

2 teaspoons baking soda

2 teaspoons ground cinnamon

6 cups (about ½ pound) finely shredded carrots

2 cups canola oil

8 large eggs

FOR THE CREAM CHEESE FROSTING

3 (8-ounce) packages cream cheese

¾ cup (1½ sticks) unsalted butter, softened

3 teaspoons pure vanilla extract, or 1 vanilla bean, scraped

6½ to 6¾ cups sifted confectioner's sugar

MAKE THE CAKE: Preheat the oven to 350°F. Butter and flour two 9-by-1½-inch round baking pans. Put the flour, sugar, baking powder, baking soda and cinnamon in the bowl of a stand mixer fitted with the paddle attachment and beat on medium speed until combined. Add the carrots, oil and eggs and beat until well combined.

Divide the batter between the two baking pans. Bake 35 to 40 minutes or until a toothpick inserted near the center of each cake comes out clean. Cool for 10 minutes in the pans, then invert the cakes onto a wire rack and let cool completely.

MAKE THE CREAM CHEESE FROSTING: In a clean mixing bowl, add the cream cheese, butter and vanilla and beat on high speed until light and fluffy. Reduce the speed to low and gradually add 2 cups confectioners' sugar, beating until well combined. Gradually beat in enough of the remaining sugar until the desired spreading consistency is reached. Cover the bowl with plastic wrap and refrigerate the frosting for at least 30 minutes and up to 1 hour to set.

LAYER AND FILL THE CAKE: With a long serrated cake knife, slice each cake horizontally in half. Put one of the cake halves rounded side up on a plate and spread the top generously with 1 cup of the confectionary dulce de leche. Continue to layer and fill the cake with

CONTINUED

FOR THE FILLING

3 cups confectionary dulce de leche, divided

Chocolate kisses, shavings of fine quality chocolate or edible flowers, for decorating the cake

the remaining cake halves and confectionary dulce de leche in the same manner, ending with a flat cake layer on the top.

FROST AND DECORATE THE CAKE: When the cream cheese frosting is set, spread it on the top and sides of the cake, covering the entire cake. Decorate as desired. Cover the cake and allow the frosting to set in the refrigerator for 30 minutes before serving. The cake keeps, covered, in the refrigerator for up to 6 days.

DEVIL'S FOOD CAKE

I first made this cake for my son Lucas' third birthday; he's now a teenager and we've been enjoying it ever since. It's irresistibly moist and chocolaty. I also keep this cake in mind for special occasions or family nights, or even to console a friend who needs cheering up. Yes, it's a bit time-consuming to make, but the payoff is big. Note that the frosting needs to chill for two hours before using, so be sure to make that first.

FOR THE CAKE

- 1 cup plus 2 tablespoons Dutch-process cocoa powder, plus extra for dusting
- 2½ cups (5 sticks) unsalted butter, softened
- 3½ cups granulated sugar
- 1½ tablespoons pure vanilla extract
- 6 large eggs, lightly beaten
- 4½ cups sifted cake flour
- 1½ teaspoons baking soda
- 1 teaspoon salt
- 1½ cups whole milk

FOR THE FROSTING

- 24 ounces semisweet chocolate morsels
- 4 cups whipping cream
- 1 teaspoon light corn syrup

FOR THE FILLING

- 3 cups confectionary dulce de leche, divided

SPECIAL EQUIPMENT

Three 9-inch round springform cake pans

MAKE THE CAKE: Preheat the oven to 350°F. Butter three 9-inch round springform cake pans and line the bottoms with parchment paper. Dust the sides of the pans with cocoa powder and tap out any excess.

Sift the cocoa powder into a medium bowl, then whisk in ¾ cup boiling water until a thick paste forms. Set aside to cool.

In a large mixing bowl, beat the butter on low speed with an electric mixer until light and fluffy. Increase the speed to medium and gradually beat in the sugar until light and fluffy, 3 to 4 minutes, scraping down the sides of the bowl twice. Beat in the vanilla. Drizzle in the eggs, a little at a time, beating after each addition and scraping down the sides of the bowl at least twice more, until the batter is no longer slick.

In a large bowl, sift together the cake flour, baking soda and salt.

Whisk the milk into the reserved cocoa paste mixture until smooth.

With the mixer on low speed, alternately add the flour and cocoa mixtures to the batter, a little at a time, beginning and ending with the flour mixture, until the batter is well combined.

Divide the batter evenly among the three baking pans. Bake 30 to 35 minutes or until a cake tester inserted into the center of each cake comes out clean. Cool for 15 minutes in the pans, then release the side of the pans and transfer cakes to wire racks, tops up and leaving the parchment paper on the bottom, and let cool completely.

CONTINUED

MAKE THE FROSTING: Put the chocolate morsels and cream in a heavy saucepan and cook over low heat, stirring constantly with a rubber spatula, until combined and thickened, 20 to 25 minutes. Increase the heat to medium low and continue to cook, stirring, 3 minutes more. Remove the pan from the heat and stir in the corn syrup. Transfer the frosting to a large metal bowl and refrigerate, covered, until cool enough to spread, about 2 hours, stirring every 15 to 20 minutes. Use immediately.

ASSEMBLE AND FILL THE CAKE: Remove the parchment from the bottoms of the cooled cakes. Reserve the prettiest cake for the top layer and, if the cakes are not flat on top, using a long serrated knife, trim the tops of the cakes. Place one cake on a serving platter to form the bottom layer. Spoon 1½ cups confectionary dulce de leche on top, then spread evenly. Add the second cake to form the second layer. Spoon the remaining 1½ cups confectionary dulce de leche on top, then spread evenly. Place the third cake to form the top layer.

As soon as the frosting is thick enough, spread it over the top and sides of the cake. The cake keeps, covered, at room temperature for up to 5 days.

CREAM-FILLED CUPCAKES
WITH CHOCOLATE BARILOCHE

Nothing tastes more like childhood to me than a good old-fashioned cupcake, and I enjoy making this indulgent version with a dulce de leche cream center. Sour cream makes the cupcakes super moist, and the smooth ganache called *chocolate Bariloche* (after the Patagonian city San Carlos de Bariloche, known for its chocolate shops) is super rich.

FOR THE CUPCAKES

1½ cups all-purpose flour

1 teaspoon baking powder

½ teaspoon baking soda

¾ cup (1½ sticks) unsalted butter, softened

1 cup granulated sugar

⅔ cup sour cream

⅓ cup unsweetened cocoa powder

2 teaspoons pure vanilla extract

2 large eggs, lightly beaten

FOR THE FILLING

1 cup heavy whipping cream

½ cup confectionary dulce de leche

MAKE THE CUPCAKES: Preheat the oven to 350°F. Line 18 cups of two muffin pans with paper liners. In a large bowl, combine the flour, baking powder and baking soda. In a bowl, beat the butter and sugar on medium-high speed with an electric mixer until well combined and creamy, about 3 minutes. In another bowl, whisk together the sour cream, cocoa powder, vanilla and eggs until combined, then add this mixture to the butter mixture and beat on medium speed until thoroughly blended. Lower the speed to low and gradually add the flour mixture, beating until just combined.

Divide the batter among the lined cups, filling each three-quarters full. Bake about 20 minutes or until a cake tester inserted into the center of the cupcakes comes out clean. Cool for 15 minutes in the pans, then invert the cupcakes onto a wire cooling rack and let cool completely. The cupcakes can be made 1 day ahead and kept in a sealed plastic bag at room temperature.

MAKE THE CREAM FILLING: Put the whipping cream in a mixing bowl and beat on high speed with an electric mixer until soft ribbons appear. Reduce the mixer speed to medium-low and add the confectionary dulce de leche in two batches, beating well after each addition until incorporated. Cover the bowl with plastic wrap and refrigerate the filling until the cupcakes are completely cool.

When the cupcakes are cool, use a thin paring knife to cut a deep,

CONTINUED

FOR THE CHOCOLATE BARILOCHE

1 cup (2 sticks) unsalted butter, softened

6 ounces 60% cacao dark chocolate, chopped

2 to 3 heaping tablespoons confectionary dulce de leche

FOR THE DECORATION

6 ounces white chocolate melting wafers

SPECIAL EQUIPMENT

Two (12-cup) muffin pans, paper cupcake liners, pastry bag with a large tip and a thin tip

narrow hole into the top of each cupcake that reaches to the center. (Reserve these crumbs for another use or for snacking.) Fill a pastry bag fitted with a large tip with the cream filling and pipe into each hole. Smooth any excess cream over the top of the cupcakes so the glaze will spread evenly over each cupcake.

MAKE THE CHOCOLATE BARILOCHE GLAZE: In a medium saucepan, combine the butter, chocolate and dulce de leche and warm over low heat, stirring constantly, until well combined and smooth. Remove the pan from the heat and let cool for just 5 minutes. The glaze will set as it cools, so don't let it cool completely.

Working quickly with one cupcake at a time, dip the top of the cupcake into the glaze to coat and return the cupcake to the cooling rack. When all the tops are coated, dip each cupcake 2 more times to create a thick glaze. Let the glaze set, about 15 minutes.

DECORATE THE CUPCAKES: Melt the white chocolate wafers in a double boiler. Remove the top pan from the heat and let the white chocolate cool until cool to the touch, about 3 minutes. Transfer the to a pastry bag fitted with a thin tip and pipe a squiggle line on top of each cupcake. Allow the decoration to set for at least 30 minutes. The cupcakes keep, covered, at room temperature for up to 3 days.

CAPPUCCINO CHEESECAKE

For the groom's cake at our wedding, I surprised Gastón with a velvety dulce de leche cheesecake with an Oreo crust. I wanted to give him and our Argentine family and guests a taste of home. This cake has a delicious surprise dulce de leche center. Like most cheesecakes, it should either be made in the early morning or the night before you plan to serve it, as it requires several hours to chill.

FOR THE CRUST

1¾ cups finely crushed graham crackers

¼ cup finely chopped pecans or walnuts

½ teaspoon ground cinnamon

½ cup (1 stick) unsalted butter, melted

FOR THE FILLING

2 (8-ounce) packages cream cheese, softened

8 ounces mascarpone cheese

1 cup granulated sugar

½ teaspoon finely ground instant espresso powder, or any instant coffee

4 large eggs, separated

2 tablespoons all-purpose flour

1¼ cups confectionary dulce de leche

Dulce de leche, whipped cream, espresso coffee beans for decorating the cheesecake, if desired

MAKE THE CRUST: Preheat the oven to 325°F. Line the bottom and sides of an 8-by-2-inch square baking pan with parchment paper, leaving an overhang to easily remove the cheesecake once chilled. In a small bowl, combine the crushed crackers, pecans and cinnamon and stir in the melted butter. Press the mixture evenly onto the bottom and sides of the pan. Bake for 10 minutes until lightly browned, then transfer the pan to a wire cooling rack and let the crust cool.

MAKE THE FILLING: Heat enough water for a hot-water bath. In a mixing bowl, combine the cream cheese, mascarpone and sugar and beat on high speed with an electric mixer until fluffy. Beat in the instant espresso powder until well combined and dissolved. Add the egg yolks, one by one, beating well after each addition. Add the flour and continue to beat until well combined.

In a separate mixing bowl, beat the egg whites on high speed with the electric mixer until soft peaks form. Gently fold the egg whites into the cheese mixture.

Put the confectionary dulce de leche in a pastry bag fitted with an extra-large tip. Pipe the dulce de leche into the center of the crust, forming a cone-like structure.

Carefully pour the filling over the dulce de leche. Place the square pan into a larger baking pan and carefully add enough boiling water to reach halfway up the sides of the square pan. Bake 1 hour or until the center of the cheesecake is nearly set when the square pan is shaken.

CONTINUED

SPECIAL EQUIPMENT

8-by-2-inch square baking
    pan (or 8-inch round pan)
    and a pastry bag fitted
    with an extra-large tip

Cool for 30 minutes in the pan on a wire rack, then refrigerate for at least 4 hours or until completely set.

If desired, decorate the top of the cheesecake with a thin layer of dulce de leche, fresh whipped cream and whole coffee beans. To serve, remove from the pan with the aid of the parchment paper and carefully transfer to a serving plate.

VARIATION: If you are not a coffee fan, substitute the beans from a scraped vanilla bean pod or 1 teaspoon orange zest for the instant espresso to change the flavor of the cheesecake.

CHOCOLATE UPSIDE-DOWN CAKE

This is an Argentine take on the pineapple upside-down cake, substituting dulce de leche for the pineapple. It may sound tricky to prepare, but it's really just physics, as the layers of chocolate cake and custardy flan trade places while baking. The cake takes on a quality all its own, and the final product is both beautiful and delicious.

FOR THE CUSTARD

4 large eggs

1 (14-ounce) can sweetened condensed milk

1 cup heavy cream

2 teaspoons pure vanilla extract

FOR THE CHOCOLATE CAKE BATTER

3 ounces 60% cacao bittersweet chocolate, chopped

1¼ cups whole milk

1½ cups (3 sticks) unsalted butter, softened

1¾ cups granulated sugar

3 large eggs

2½ cups all-purpose flour

1½ tablespoons baking powder

2 cups traditional dulce de leche

SPECIAL EQUIPMENT

10-inch tube pan

Preheat the oven to 325°F. Butter a 10-inch tube pan and dust with flour.

MAKE THE CUSTARD: In a blender, combine the eggs, sweetened condensed milk, cream and vanilla and blend until smooth. Set aside.

MAKE THE CHOCOLATE CAKE BATTER: Put the chocolate in a medium heatproof bowl. In a small saucepan over medium-high heat, bring ½ cup of the milk just to a boil and pour over the chocolate, stirring until melted.

Put the butter and sugar in the bowl of an electric mixer fitted with the paddle attachment and beat on medium speed until light and fluffy, about 3 minutes. Add the eggs, one at a time, beating after each addition until well incorporated. Pour the egg mixture into the melted chocolate and stir until combined.

In a medium bowl, whisk together the flour and baking powder, then whisk the mixture into the batter in two batches, alternating with the remaining ¾ cup milk. Continue to whisk the batter until smooth and fluffy, about 3 more minutes.

Pour the dulce de leche into the bottom of the tube pan and spread evenly. Pour in the chocolate batter and tap the pan on a work surface to spread the batter evenly to the edges. Very carefully, pour the custard mixture evenly over the top.

BAKE THE CAKE: Boil enough water for a hot-water bath. Set the tube pan into a deep baking pan and fill the baking pan with enough boiling water to reach a third of the way up the sides of the tube pan.

CONTINUED

Bake the cake for 1 hour and 20 minutes or until a toothpick inserted in the center comes out clean. Remove the tube pan from the hot-water bath and let cool for 30 minutes in the pan on a wire rack.

While still slightly warm, place an inverted serving plate on top of the tube pan. Using two hands to anchor the plate and pan together, carefully flip it over. Let the cake rest upside-down in the pan on the plate for 30 minutes in the refrigerator to allow the dulce de leche to release and drip over the cake. Gently shake the pan and plate together to help unmold the cake, but be careful not to break the flan, as it is very delicate. Remove the pan and refrigerate the cake for at least 30 minutes before serving.

OLGA'S ALFAJOR LAYER CAKE

Olga, my mom's best friend, is Peruvian, so she fills her alfajor cake with homemade *manjar blanco* (white delicacy), a thicker cousin to Argentina's traditional dulce de leche and more similar to *el repostero* (confectionary dulce de leche). My Argentine version is rustic yet delicate, with the perfect balance of crunchy shortbread and silken dulce de leche. Although you can drench the cake in chocolate (see Variation), I prefer it plain, with a dusting of confectioners' sugar that leaves the layers of dulce de leche visible. *¡Diez puntos!* (Perfection!)

4 cups all-purpose flour

8 tablespoons confectioners' sugar

1½ cups (3 sticks) unsalted butter, softened

½ cup milk

4 cups confectionary dulce de leche

SPECIAL EQUIPMENT
Six baking sheets

Preheat the oven to 350°F. In a large bowl, whisk together the flour and confectioners' sugar until combined. Using a fork, press in the butter, one stick at a time, alternately adding the milk, until a dough is formed. Turn out the dough onto a floured surface and knead just until a soft silky texture is reached. Shape into a log and cut into 6 equal pieces.

Line 6 baking sheets with parchment paper. On a well-floured surface, roll out one piece of dough into a paper-thin round, slightly larger than the diameter of a 7-inch dinner plate, making sure it doesn't stick to the work surface. Lightly place the dinner plate, face down, on the dough and trace around the plate with the point of a knife to form a perfect circle. With a rolling pin, transfer the dough round very carefully to the parchment lined baking sheet. Make more circles in the same manner with the 5 remaining pieces of dough.

Bake each round for 12 to 15 minutes or until the edges are a light golden brown. Transfer the round carefully on the parchment to a rack and let cool completely. (Use the parchment to move and handle the rounds, as they are very delicate.)

When all the rounds are cool, layer the cake by placing one round on a platter. Using an offset spatula, very gently spread a generous layer of confectionary dulce de leche on top to cover completely. (Use a light touch, because the cake is very fragile and can easily crumble.) Continue to layer and fill the cake in the same manner with the remaining rounds and dulce de leche. Sprinkle the top layer of dulce de

CONTINUED

leche with some confectioners' sugar.

VARIATION: If you prefer, you can cover this cake with a velvety chocolate ganache. To make the ganache, coarsely chop 6 ounces of 60% cacao chocolate and set aside. In a saucepan, heat ½ cup heavy whipping cream over medium heat until bubbles form around the edges of the pan. Pour into a large bowl and let cool for 1 minute.

Meanwhile, fill a second, larger bowl with hot water (not steaming). Add all the chocolate to the hot cream, then place the bowl over the hot water and stir until fully melted and well combined. Add 4 tablespoons of softened unsalted butter and mix until combined. Strain the chocolate ganache through a fine-mesh sieve into a small bowl.

Pour the ganache over the alfajor cake, allowing it to drip over the sides. To maintain its shine, do not spread the ganache. Let set at room temperature for at least 1 hour prior to cutting into the cake.

PUMPKIN PIONONO

The beauty of an *arrollado* (rolled cake) is that it looks impressive, but it's actually quite simple to make. The *pionono*, named after Pope Pius IX's Italian name, *Pio Nono*, is Argentina's flagship jelly roll that can be made sweet or savory. Mixing the batter is quick and easy, and the cake only bakes for fifteen minutes. And unlike a layer cake, there is no work slicing it into layers, filling, frosting or decorating. Be careful not to use too much filling (I've been guilty of this), as it will be harder to roll.

FOR THE CAKE

¾ cup all-purpose flour

1 cup granulated sugar

1 teaspoon baking soda

½ teaspoon ground cinnamon

Pinch of salt

⅔ cup canned pumpkin

1 cup canola oil

3 large eggs

Confectioners' sugar

FOR THE FILLING

1½ cups confectionary dulce de leche

1 (8-ounce) package cream cheese, softened

¼ cup (½ stick) unsalted butter, softened

SPECIAL EQUIPMENT

15¼-by-10¼-by-¾-inch rimmed baking sheet, a towel or cheesecloth (for rolling the cake)

MAKE THE CAKE: Preheat the oven to 375°F. Butter a 15¼-by-10¼-by-¾-inch rimmed baking sheet, then line with parchment paper and butter the paper. In a large bowl, sift together the flour, sugar, baking soda, cinnamon and salt. In another bowl, stir together the pumpkin and canola oil, then add the eggs, one at a time, stirring until each to incorporate before adding the next and scraping down the sides of the bowl with a spatula. Slowly stir in the flour mixture just until thoroughly combined. Pour the batter into the baking sheet and bake for 15 minutes or until a toothpick inserted near the center comes out clean.

On a work surface, place a large towel or cheesecloth that is slightly larger than the baking sheet and, using a sifter, lightly sprinkle with confectioners' sugar to keep the towel from sticking to the cake. Invert the hot cake onto the towel and peel off the parchment paper. Starting with a long side, roll up the cake in the towel, jelly-roll fashion, and let cool for 1 hour.

MEANWHILE, MAKE THE FILLING: Put the dulce de leche, cream cheese and butter in a mixing bowl and beat on medium speed with an electric mixer until creamy.

Unroll the cake. Evenly spread the filling over the cake, leaving a ½-inch border on all sides. Using the towel as a guide and starting with a long side, roll up the cake around the filling, jelly-roll fashion. Sprinkle lightly with confectioners' sugar. The cake keeps, tightly covered, in the refrigerator, for up to 5 days.

DULCE DE LECHE TIRAMISÙ

As a crew of six kids, we would fly through any snacks Mom brought home from the grocery store in a day or two before considering her stash of Italian ladyfingers in the back of the pantry—a last resort. Invariably, the day before one of her dinner parties, she would go to make her tiramisù and the ladyfingers would be half gone!

It's always best to make this simple, indulgent dessert the day before you'll be serving it to allow the liqueur and coffee to soak into the cake.

6 large egg yolks, room temperature

¼ cup granulated sugar

½ cup Cointreau or premium barrel rum, divided

1½ cups brewed espresso at room temperature, divided

12 ounces mascarpone cheese

1¼ cup confectionary dulce de leche, divided

Zest of 1 lemon

1 large package (500 grams) Italian ladyfingers

2 cups whipping cream

Bittersweet chocolate, shaved or grated

Butter a 13-by-9-by-2-inch baking pan or glass dish, then line with parchment and butter the paper. Put the egg yolks and sugar in the bowl of a stand mixer fitted with the whisk attachment and whisk on high speed for 5 minutes until very thick and pale yellow. Reduce the speed to medium and add ¼ cup of the liqueur, ¼ cup espresso, the cheese, 1 cup dulce de leche and the lemon zest, whisking until smooth.

In a shallow bowl, combine the remaining ¼ cup liqueur and 1¼ cups espresso. Put 3 tablespoons of the mixture in a small bowl and reserve for the whipped cream topping. Working with one ladyfinger at a time, dip one side of each quickly in the remaining coffee-liqueur mixture and then place in the bottom of the baking dish, soaked side up, until the entire pan is lined with the ladyfingers. Spread half of the mascarpone mixture evenly on top. Repeat this process for a second layer, spreading the remaining mascarpone mixture over the second layer of dipped ladyfingers. Add a third layer of dipped ladyfingers.

Put the whipping cream in a clean bowl of the stand mixer fitted with a clean whisk attachment and whisk on high speed until soft peaks form. Add the remaining ¼ cup of dulce de leche and 3 tablespoons of the coffee-liqueur mixture and continue to whisk until thick. Spread the flavored whipped cream evenly over the top layer of dipped ladyfingers, cover with plastic wrap and refrigerate overnight.

When ready to serve, sprinkle the top with the shaved chocolate. Holding the sides of the parchment paper, carefully transfer the tiramisù from the baking pan to a serving tray. With the tip of a sharp knife, trim the parchment around the base of the cake. To garnish, use a vegetable peeler to shave decorative curls of chocolate on top.

VARIATION: During the holidays, my mother would make two separate pans of tiramisù–one for the adults and a hot chocolate one with less coffee and no booze for the children. Truthfully, there is such a small amount of liqueur in the recipe that anyone can eat this, but some don't like the taste. I also use decaf espresso, when possible.

For the virgin chocolate tiramisù, prepare the mascarpone mixture as above but leave out the liqueur. Then substitute 1½ cups of a high-quality dark hot chocolate prepared with water (not milk) for the coffee-liqueur mixture that is used to dip the ladyfingers. When making the whipped cream topping, substitute 1 tablespoon cocoa powder for the coffee-liqueur mixture. Tiramisù keeps, covered, in the refrigerator for up to 3 days.

FLOURLESS CHOCOLATE-ESPRESSO CAKE

This is a nice choice for a dinner party. It's super light and airy, although due to the lack of flour, it will sink once you take it out of the oven. Don't worry! The billowy whipped mixture of cream cheese, dulce de leche and espresso will cover any imperfections. Note that it requires several hours of chilling before you serve it. Serve with a good Argentine Malbec.

FOR THE CAKE

8 ounces 60% cacao semisweet chocolate

5½ tablespoons unsalted butter, cut into cubes

5 large eggs, separated

½ cup granulated sugar

FOR THE FROSTING

12 ounces cream cheese, softened

1¼ cups confectionary dulce de leche

4 teaspoons fresh-brewed espresso, at room temperature

1 teaspoon granulated sugar

Unsweetened cocoa powder, for decorating the cake

SPECIAL EQUIPMENT

9-inch springform pan

MAKE THE CAKE: Preheat the oven to 350°F. Butter and flour a 9-inch springform pan and line bottom and sides with parchment paper. In the top of a double boiler over simmering water, melt the chocolate and butter together, stirring until smooth. Remove the top pan from the heat and set aside for 5 minutes to cool.

In a mixing bowl, beat the egg whites with the sugar over high speed with an electric mixer until stiff peaks form.

When the chocolate mixture is cool, add the egg yolks, one by one, whisking vigorously after each addition until each is incorporated before adding the next. Gently fold in the egg whites until well combined. Pour the batter into the baking pan. Bake 20 to 25 minutes or until the center is set. Transfer the cake in the pan to a wire cooling rack and let cool for at least 1 hour.

MAKE THE FROSTING: In a mixing bowl, beat the cream cheese and confectionary dulce de leche on high speed with an electric mixer until smooth and well combined. Reduce the speed to low and beat in the espresso and sugar.

Spoon the frosting onto the top of the cake and spread until smooth. Refrigerate the cake in the baking pan, covered with aluminum foil, for at least 4 hours, to set.

To serve, remove sides of the cake pan. Using a fine-mesh sieve, dust the top of the cake with a thin layer of unsweetened cocoa powder.

DULCE DE LECHE FLAN

Flan is a humble Argentine staple that celebrates everyday ingredients. It is typically served with a dollop of whipped cream or dulce de leche, or both (*flan mixto*). It is the simplest of desserts. Refrigerating the flan overnight while inverted is a trick my mother-in-law taught me that ensures that all the caramel will release from the pan and drip down over the flan. While this recipe should make twelve servings, in my house it's only good for seven.

FOR THE CUSTARD

4 cups whole milk

1 cup confectionary dulce de leche

10 large eggs

1 teaspoon pure vanilla extract

FOR THE CARAMEL

1 cup granulated sugar

Traditional dulce de leche and whipped cream, for garnish

SPECIAL EQUIPMENT

10-inch tube pan (4½ inches deep, without a removable bottom) and a pastry brush

Preheat the oven to 350°F.

MAKE THE CUSTARD: Put the milk and confectionary dulce de leche in the bowl of a stand mixer fitted with a whisk attachment and beat on medium speed until blended. Add the eggs, one at a time, beating until each egg is incorporated before adding the next. Beat in the vanilla.

MAKE THE CARAMEL AND COAT THE PAN: In a small saucepan, stir together the sugar and ¼ cup water (just enough to cover the surface of the sugar) over medium heat and bring to a boil. Reduce the heat to medium-low and cook at a slow boil, untouched, for about 10 more minutes or until the mixture takes on a golden caramel color. Remove the pan from the heat and let cool. Once cool to the touch, use a pastry brush to cover the entire interior of a 10-inch tube pan with the caramel.

BAKE THE FLAN: Boil enough water for a hot-water bath. Pour the custard into the caramel-coated tube pan. Set the tube pan in a deep baking pan and fill the baking pan with enough boiling water to reach a third of the way up the side of the tube pan. Bake for 1 hour or until a knife inserted in the center comes out clean.

Remove the tube pan from the hot-water bath. Cool for 30 minutes in the pan on a wire cooling rack, then refrigerate, inverted, while still in the pan. Place an inverted serving plate on top of the tube pan. Using two hands to anchor the pan and plate together, carefully flip it over, allowing the pan to rest upside-down on the plate. Refrigerate for at

CONTINUED

least four hours, preferably overnight. This will ensure the caramel releases entirely from the pan and drips over the flan.

When ready to serve, gently shake the pan and plate together to help unmold the flan, but be cautious to not break the flan, as it is very delicate. Remove the pan and garnish the flan with traditional dulce de leche and fresh whipped cream.

DULCE DE LECHE CRÈME BRULÉE

My mom and I always loved crème brulée. If it was on the menu at a restaurant, we knew without discussion we'd be sharing it. I now share it with my children; of course, they usually eat the entire burnt sugar layer, leaving me the custard, which is okay by me. This really is an easy dessert, especially if you don't like to bake. And no worries—if you don't own a kitchen torch to caramelize the sugar, pop the custards under the broiler for about a minute, then serve them hot with whipped cream, strawberries and some fresh basil or mint.

4 cups heavy whipping cream

1¼ cups granulated sugar, divided, plus additional for the topping

1½ teaspoons pure vanilla extract

1½ cups traditional dulce de leche

11 large egg yolks

Fresh berries and whipped cream

SPECIAL EQUIPMENT

Ten (7-ounce) ramekins (5 inches in diameter, about 1 inch deep)

Preheat the oven to 325°F. In a large saucepan combine the cream, ½ cup plus 2 tablespoons of the sugar, the vanilla extract and the traditional dulce de leche and heat the mixture over medium heat just until it steams (do not let boil). Remove the pan from the heat.

Put the egg yolks and remaining ¾ cup plus 2 tablespoons sugar in the bowl of a stand mixer fitted with the paddle attachment and beat on high speed until the mixture is light in texture and pale yellow, 5 to 7 minutes. Reduce the speed to low and very slowly pour the hot cream, a little bit at a time, into the egg and sugar mixture, beating until the batter becomes smooth and fully combined. Pour the mixture through a fine-mesh sieve into a bowl to eliminate any lumps.

Pour the batter into the ramekins, dividing it evenly. Working near the oven, place the ramekins in a deep baking pan and carefully pour enough boiling water into the pan and around the ramekins to create steam. Cover the pan with foil, place in the oven and bake for about 50 minutes or until the mixture is set. Cool completely, then refrigerate, covered with plastic wrap, for at least 30 minutes and up to 2 days.

Before serving, lightly sprinkle the tops of the custards with sugar, shaking off excess, and caramelize with a kitchen torch, or place the ramekins under a preheated broiler for about 1 minute, until browned. Serve with fresh berries and whipped cream.

The Wisdom of Dorita

FOR AS LONG AS I CAN REMEMBER, I have found solace in baking. It has something to do with my love for all things dulce de leche and dark chocolate, but it goes beyond that. Whether late at night or on Sundays when I routinely bake all afternoon, it is in the kitchen where I get back to being me. The process of weighing out butter and sugar, whisking eggs, beating and folding–it all creates a mindfulness that takes me back into the kitchen with my mother and grandma Dorita.

I'm reminded of the hundreds of *tartas* laden with fruits, *crema chantilly* (whipped cream) and dulce de leche they made for me throughout my life. I hear Dorita saying, "One more finger of *leche, querida,* otherwise your dough will crack on you." And my mom chiming in, *"Vamos Mamá, cuando hay hambre no hay pan duro."* ("Come on, Mom, even stale bread tastes good when you're hungry.") Mom never was much of a baker, so she wasn't nearly as worried about perfection.

It's easy to imagine why *postre* (dessert) mattered so much to my grandma. *La charla* (conversation), she'd say, always grows more engaging over a *cafecito con algo dulce* (coffee with a little something sweet). Dorita's favorite dessert was *flan mixto* (crème caramel custard), served with a generous dollop of whipped cream and dulce de leche. It was one of the first desserts she taught me to bake as a child and her way of passing on her Argentine roots. I remember that she praised me by saying, *"¡Te salió bárbaro el flan!"* ("It turned out great, Jose!")

PANQUEUES FLAMBEADOS AL RON

This show-stopping dessert is on every Argentine steakhouse menu that serves *asado*. The crêpes are usually flambéed with rum and caramelized sugar, oozing with melted dulce de leche. Flambéing at home may seem intimidating, but it really is simple and allows you to create a dramatic effect while adding liqueur flavor without the alcohol. I like to flambé the *panqueques* in smaller batches to thoroughly caramelize each one; they tend to get soggy if made in large batches. Of course, you may choose to skip the flambé and serve them with whipped cream instead. Any which way, they are a treat.

FOR THE *PANQUEUES*

3 large eggs

2 cups whole milk

1 cup all-purpose flour, preferably unbleached

¼ teaspoon salt

4 tablespoons unsalted butter, melted, plus more for coating the pan

2 tablespoons granulated sugar

FOR THE FILLING AND FLAMBÉ

2 cups confectionary dulce de leche

4 teaspoons light brown sugar

1 cup premium barrel rum

1 pint vanilla ice cream, for serving

PREPARE THE *PANQUEUES*: Put the eggs, milk, flour, salt, melted butter and sugar in a blender and blend for 30 seconds or until smooth. Scrape down the sides and repeat, if necessary. Cover and refrigerate for at least 1 hour (2 hours is preferable) and up to 24 hours.

If the chilled batter has separated, gently stir it until it comes back together. Lightly butter a 6- or 7-inch nonstick pan and heat over medium-high heat until hot. Lift the pan from the heat and pour in 2 to 3 tablespoons of batter, tilting and rotating the pan to coat the surface. Return the pan to the heat and cook until almost dry on top and lightly browned on the edges, about 1 minute. Loosen the edges with a spatula and, using your fingers or a spatula, flip over the *panqueque* and cook the other side for about 15 seconds or until lightly browned.

Repeat with the remaining batter in the same manner, coating the pan with butter (we peel back the paper on the stick of butter and wipe it on the pan) as needed, and stacking the *panqueques* after they are cooked. (The stack of *panqueques* can be kept, wrapped in plastic wrap and refrigerated, for up to 3 days.) Fill with dulce de leche just before serving.

FILL AND FOLD THE *PANQUEUES*: Place a *panqueque* on a work surface and thinly spread some of the confectionary dulce de leche

CONTINUED

Flambé pan, large skillet or large chafing dish with rounded, deep sides and a long handle; gas stovetop or kitchen torch

over half of it. Fold each in half over the dulce de leche, then fold in half again to form a wedge shape. Fill and fold the remaining *panqueques* in the same manner.

PREPARE THE RANGE FOR FLAMBÉING: Turn off the other burners and your stove's overhead fan or hood. Arrange 4 folded *panqueques* around the edge of a 10-inch nonstick skillet with high sides. Sprinkle evenly with ¼ teaspoon light brown sugar. Using a spoon (and not directly from the bottle), add 4 tablespoons of the rum to the skillet and heat over medium heat just until bubbles begin to form around the edges. Do not bring the rum to a boil, as it will burn off the alcohol and will not ignite.

Use a long utility lighter to ignite the rum. Using two long-handled metal spoons, carefully move the *panqueques* so they are surrounded by the flames to evenly heat them through and caramelize the sugar on top, about 30 seconds.

Alternately, you can skip the rum, lightly sprinkle with sugar and caramelize with a kitchen torch.

Transfer to individual plates and serve immediately with vanilla ice cream, if desired, passing any extra pan sauce. Flambé and serve the remaining *panqueques* in the same manner.

PEARS WRAPPED IN FILO

Just about anything wrapped in flaky pastry looks impressive and is fun to eat, so I always keep a box of frozen Greek filo dough in the freezer for last-minute invitations or surprise guests. This little dessert gives a regal yet rustic appearance that belies its simplicity.

16 sheets filo pastry, defrosted if frozen

4 firm ripe pears, preferably Bartlett

3 tablespoons unsalted butter, melted

¾ cup confectionary dulce de leche

1 teaspoon ground cinnamon

2 teaspoons granulated sugar

4 teaspoons raw natural slivered almonds

French vanilla ice cream, whipped cream or mascarpone cheese, as an accompaniment

SPECIAL EQUIPMENT

Pastry bag fitted with a medium-sized tip

Preheat the oven to 325°F. Line a baking sheet with parchment paper. Cover the stack of filo with a slightly damp towel to prevent it from becoming brittle.

Carefully peel the pears with a vegetable peeler and carve out the cores from the bottom, leaving the stems intact. This will give you a generous-sized hole to fill.

Working with one piece of filo at a time and keeping the remaining dough covered, brush the top of one filo sheet with some melted butter, then continue to layer and butter with three more sheets until you have a stack of four.

Fill a pastry bag fitted with a medium-sized tip with the dulce de leche, then fill one pear generously with it, leaving excess around the bottom of the pear. Place the filled pear in the middle of the filo stack, then gather up the filo around the stem and pinch tightly, folding over the excess. Transfer the prepared pear to a plate. Fill and wrap the remaining three pears in the same manner and transfer to the plate. Once all the pears are prepared, brush the pastry with any remaining melted butter.

Combine the cinnamon and sugar in a small bowl and sprinkle over the tops of the pears, then sprinkle each pear with 1 teaspoon of slivered almonds. Place the pears on the baking sheet and bake for 25 to 30 minutes until the pastry is golden and crisp. Serve immediately with ice cream, whipped cream or mascarpone cheese.

DEEP-DISH PEACH TART

This is one of Gastón's favorite desserts. He particularly likes the tender, thick dough and the way the syrup from the peaches pools into the dulce de leche and just melts in your mouth. Don't be put off by the jarred peaches! They are beautiful, easy to handle and taste great.

FOR THE DOUGH

2 to 2½ cups unbleached self-rising flour

1 large egg

1 large egg yolk

1 cup granulated sugar

½ cup unsalted butter, chilled

1 to 2 tablespoons 2% or whole milk

FOR THE TOPPING

12 ounces confectionary dulce de leche

1 (29-ounce) jar of peach halves in light or heavy syrup, drained

½ cup walnut halves (optional)

SPECIAL EQUIPMENT

12-inch deep-dish tart pan

MAKE THE DOUGH: Put the flour, egg and egg yolk, sugar, butter and milk into a food processor and pulse until the dough forms pea-size lumps. Turn the dough out onto a work surface. With floured hands, gently knead the dough just until moist. Add additional flour or drops of milk as needed to reach a smooth consistency. Lightly flour the top of the dough and form into a round. Place it on a small baking sheet and refrigerate, loosely covered with plastic wrap, for 30 minutes.

Preheat the oven to 350°F. Butter the bottom and sides of a 12-inch deep-dish tart pan and line with parchment paper. Press the dough evenly into the bottom and sides of the pan. Bake the tart shell for 25 to 30 minutes until golden brown. Cool for 10 minutes in the pan, then remove the shell carefully from the pan with the aid of the parchment and transfer to a rack to cool completely.

FILL THE TART: When the tart shell is completely cool, use a spatula and spread the bottom with a generous layer of the confectionary dulce de leche. Arrange the peach halves, cut sides down, on top and sprinkle with the walnuts, if desired. The tart, covered with plastic wrap, can be kept in the refrigerator for up to 5 days.

VARIATION: For a *frutas del bosque* tart, substitute 1 pint each fresh blueberries, raspberries and strawberries (hulled and halved) for the peaches and prepare as above. Arrange the berries over the dulce de leche in a circular pattern. Begin with a row of strawberries along the outer edge, then a row of blueberries stacked high and finally a row of raspberries. Repeat until the tart is fully covered with the berries, or leave some of the dulce de leche showing in the center.

PASTAFROLA

Like many classic Argentine recipes, *pastafrola* is Italian in origin and consists of a shortbread-like dough (*pasta frolla*) that is used in a variety of cakes and cookies. In Argentina, *pastafrola* refers specifically to a dessert with a lattice crust, filled with dulce de leche, *dulce de membrillo* (quince jam) or any other filling. Here it takes the form of a tart. It's easy and fast and can be made with any prepared filling that you have on hand.

3½ cups all-purpose flour

½ cup granulated sugar

1 teaspoon baking powder

10 tablespoons cold unsalted butter, cut into small cubes

1 large egg

2 large egg yolks

1 teaspoon pure vanilla extract

1½ cups confectionary dulce de leche

SPECIAL EQUIPMENT

9½-inch round tart pan with a removable bottom

Preheat the oven to 350°F. Butter and flour a 9½-inch round tart pan with a removable bottom. On a clean work surface, mix together the flour, sugar and baking powder. Add the butter cubes and, working quickly with a fork or two knives, cut the butter into the flour mixture until it is incorporated and resembles coarse sand.

With your hands, make a well in the flour mixture. Add the egg yolks and the vanilla to the well and mix them into the flour in a circular motion with your hand, adding 2 to 3 tablespoons of water if necessary, until a dough is formed. (The dough should not be too dry, crumbling apart or sticky.) Form the dough into a ball and let rest in a cool place for 10 to 20 minutes under a damp cloth.

On a floured surface, roll out the dough into a 12-inch round and put it into the tart pan to cover the bottom and the sides. Pat the dough into the pan to cover it completely and leave some extra around the edges to form a crust. Carefully spread the dulce de leche over the dough. Roll out the dough scraps and, with a pastry cutter or knife, cut into ½-inch strips. Lay the strips across the top of the filling in a lattice pattern. Whisk the remaining egg with a bit of water and brush the egg wash on the edge and strips of the tart to create a shiny finish.

Bake for 40 to 45 minutes until golden on the top. Cool completely on a wire rack. The dulce de leche filling will set as the tart cools.

HELADO
DE DULCE DE LECHE

Argentina's artisanal ice cream is a legacy of Italian immigrants who came to the country in two waves: first in the late 1800s with the general migration of Europeans to the New World, and again in the 1940s after World War II, bringing with them not only Italian gelato recipes but also the *heladería* culture. Today, ice cream parlors can be found on every other block in Buenos Aires. Summer nights find *heladerías* nearly as packed as the bars, and open just as late. It is some of the best ice cream in the world.

This recipe is the closest I've come to reproducing it. An endless array of toppings can be mixed into this ice cream; *granizado* (chocolate chunks) and chopped pistachios are my favorites. Serve it in Meringue Cones (page 171).

1½ cups whole milk

1½ cups heavy cream

6 large egg yolks

2¼ cups dulce de leche—traditional, confectionary or dark chocolate

Optional mix-ins: Dark chocolate chunks, chopped pistachios or sea salt

SPECIAL EQUIPMENT

Ice cream maker (Place its bowl in freezer at least 8 hours before using)

In a 3-quart heavy saucepan, stir together the milk and cream and bring just to a boil over moderate heat, stirring constantly. Remove from the heat and let rest for 5 minutes.

In a medium bowl, whisk the egg yolks, then whisk in a small amount of the hot cream mixture to temper the yolks and keep them from curdling. Gradually add the tempered yolks to the hot cream mixture, whisking constantly. Once the yolks are fully incorporated, return the saucepan to the stove over medium-low heat and stir the mixture constantly with a wooden spoon until the custard coats the back of the spoon, about 5 minutes. Do not let the mixture boil. Strain through a fine-mesh sieve into a clean bowl to remove any bits of cooked yolk. Whisk in the dulce de leche of your choice until dissolved.

Quick-chill the custard by putting the bowl in a larger bowl of ice and cold water and stirring occasionally until cold, 15 to 20 minutes. When cool to the touch, cover with foil and put in the refrigerator for 2 to 3 hours to thoroughly chill before churning. Freeze the custard mixture in an ice cream maker until almost firm, then fold in the mix-ins of choice or leave plain. If you are making the salted dulce de leche version, use ¾ teaspoon finely ground sea salt. Transfer the ice cream to an airtight container and freeze to harden for at least 1 hour and up to 2 weeks.

MERINGUE CONES

An elegant way to serve ice cream, and since the recipe for dulce de leche ice cream calls for so many egg yolks, you get to use up all those leftover egg whites. These aren't true cones; they're shaped like shells.

4 large egg whites
¼ teaspoon salt
¼ teaspoon cream of tartar
1½ cups granulated sugar

Preheat the oven to 180°F. Line a baking sheet with parchment paper. Put the egg whites in the bowl of a stand mixer fitted with the whisk attachment and beat on medium speed until foamy. Add the salt and cream of tartar and continue to whisk until soft peaks form. Slowly whisk in the sugar, then increase the speed to high and whisk until the mixture is thick and shiny, about 2 minutes.

Create the meringue shells, one at a time, directly on the parchment-lined baking sheet. Place ½ cup of meringue in a mound. Using a wet spoon, make a depression in the center about 3 inches wide (big enough to hold a large scoop of ice cream). Be sure to leave at least ¼ inch of meringue on the bottom of the shell. Make more shells in the same manner on the baking sheet. (Note: The meringue will not spread during baking, so place them close together to fit all the shells on one sheet.)

Bake the shells for 3 hours. The meringues are done when pale golden in color and fairly crisp. Turn off the oven and prop open the door, letting the meringues sit there until cool, about 1 hour. The meringues keep, in an airtight container, up to 5 days.

VARIATION: For chocolate chip meringues, mix ¾ cup miniature chocolate chips into the meringue just before creating the shells.

LEMON ICEBOX PIE

Ever since our Southern friends Lark and Hunter introduced us to lemon icebox cake—an American classic that's been around since World War I and grew very popular in the 1920s and '30s with commercial shortcuts and premade ingredients—there's been no turning back. I was hooked from the first bite but prefer the simplicity of the pie version (to make an icebox cake, just use a springform pan). The addition of dulce de leche to the filling is my own twist; to my mind, it balances the tartness of the lemons.

FOR THE CRUST

1 (30-ounce) box vanilla wafers

3 tablespoons unsalted butter, melted

FOR THE FILLING

6 large egg yolks

2 (14-ounce) cans sweetened condensed milk

½ cup confectionary dulce de leche

1 cup plus 1 tablespoon freshly squeezed lemon juice, strained (from about 6 large lemons)

FOR THE TOPPING

1 cup heavy whipping cream

2 tablespoons confectioners' sugar

Dulce de leche, for drizzling

Lemon slices and fresh mint leaves, for garnish

SPECIAL EQUIPMENT

10-inch pie pan

MAKE THE CRUST: Preheat the oven to 350°F. Lightly coat a 10-inch pie pan with nonstick cooking spray. Put the cookies in a food processor and pulse until finely crushed. Add the melted butter and process until thoroughly combined. Press the crumb mixture evenly into the pie dish, pressing on the bottom, up the sides and onto the lip of the dish. Bake for 10 minutes. Let the shell cool on a wire rack for 30 minutes.

MAKE THE FILLING: In a large bowl, whisk together the egg yolks, sweetened condensed milk, confectionary dulce de leche and lemon juice until well combined and pour into the cooled shell. Bake the pie for 15 minutes or until almost set but the center jiggles slightly. Transfer to a wire rack and let cool completely, about 1 hour. Cover and refrigerate for at least 8 hours and up to 2 days.

MAKE THE TOPPING: In a medium bowl, beat the cream on high speed with an electric mixer until foamy. Reduce the speed to medium-low and gradually add the confectioners' sugar, then increase the speed to high and continue beating until soft peaks form. Dollop the sweetened cream over the chilled pie and drizzle dulce de leche over the top. Garnish with lemon slices and mint.

CORONA DE REINA

This stunning dulce de leche banana cream pie is named after the queen's crown, due to its form and majesty. Shortly after meeting Gastón, he affectionately nicknamed me *Reina* (Queen); I am pretty sure it is meant affectionately—most of the time. From a casual wedding to a Sunday dinner, this masterpiece promises to set the mood for any important gathering.

I dedicate this cake to the queen in all of us. May we celebrate her often.

FOR THE SHORT-CRUST PASTRY

4½ cups all-purpose flour

¾ cup granulated sugar

Pinch of salt

1¼ cups unsalted butter, at room temperature

1 large egg

1 large egg yolk

FOR THE FILLING

¾ cup heavy whipping cream

4 large bananas

1¼ cup confectionary dulce de leche

Banana slices and edible flowers, for garnish (optional)

SPECIAL EQUIPMENT

9-by-1½-inch springform pan and pastry bag with a medium-sized star tip

MAKE THE SHORT-CRUST PASTRY: In a large bowl, combine the flour, sugar and salt. Using a fork or your fingers, cut in the butter until pea-size lumps form. Make a well in the center and add the egg and egg yolk. With a wooden spoon, gradually incorporate the egg into the flour mixture, slowly adding up to 3 tablespoons of water, just until a ball forms.

Turn the dough out onto a work surface, and knead until just combined and smooth in texture. Wrap in plastic wrap and let rest in the refrigerator for 20 minutes.

While the dough chills, preheat the oven to 350°F. Butter and flour a 9-by-1½-inch springform pan.

Press the chilled dough evenly onto the bottom and two-thirds of the way up the side of the springform pan. Bake for 10 minutes. Remove the pan from the oven, and with the back of a fork, press the sides of the tender dough up towards the top of the pan to create a "queen's crown." Return the pan to the oven and bake for another 5 minutes. Remove the pan from the oven, and with the back of the fork, press the sides of the dough up towards the top of the pan again. Return the pan to the oven and bake for 10 to 15 minutes more until golden brown. Cool for least 30 minutes in the pan on a rack before filling.

MAKE THE FILLING: In a medium bowl, beat the cream on high speed with an electric mixer until soft peaks form. In a blender, purée the bananas until smooth. Gently fold the bananas into the whipped cream

CONTINUED

and pour the filling into the cooled crust. Let the pie chill in the freezer for at least 1 hour or until the filling is set.

Using a pastry bag fitted with a medium-sized star tip, lavishly decorate the top with confectionary dulce de leche rosettes, or using an offset cake spatula, spread the dulce de leche evenly over the top.

To serve, carefully remove the sides of the pan and garnish with banana slices and/or edible flowers, if desired. The pie keeps, covered, in the refrigerator for up to 5 days.

TOASTED COCONUT COFFEE TRUFAS

My sister-in-law Micaela taught me how to make these truffles. They're so simple—yet so decadent—that I almost feel like I am fooling my guests. If I were to tell them I slaved away in the kitchen, I'm sure they'd believe me! Since the recipe makes so many truffles, you might want to vary them with your favorite flavorings and coatings (see Variations below).

10 tablespoons unsalted butter, at room temperature

4 tablespoons traditional dulce de leche

1 teaspoon finely ground instant coffee

3½ cups finely ground crumbs of biscotti, Italian ladyfingers or biscuit crackers

Toasted shredded coconut, for rolling

SPECIAL EQUIPMENT

Mini paper baking cups

Line a baking sheet with parchment paper.

In a mixing bowl, beat together the butter, dulce de leche and instant coffee on medium speed with an electric mixer until combined, then mix in the ground biscotti crumbs until completely incorporated and a dough forms. With a small spoon and your hands, form the mixture into 1-inch balls and place on the baking sheet.

Put the toasted coconut in a small shallow bowl. Roll the balls, one at a time, in the coconut, and place in paper mini baking cups. If the coconut does not stick, spread a thin layer of dulce de leche on the surface of each truffle before rolling again.

VARIATIONS: These truffles can be rolled in anything your heart desires: pulverized almonds, confectioners' sugar and unsweetened cocoa are great options, and my kids like chocolate jimmies. For more elegant affairs, finish them off with edible shimmery gold dust.

CHOCOLATE TORTUGAS

Whimsical and fun to make, these little confections are a lighter-textured version of the traditional pecan turtles. The combination of toasted pecans and dulce de leche enveloped in smooth dark chocolate is impossible to resist. This rendition takes a bit longer than most turtle recipes, as the chocolate must be given time to set twice, but it's worth it.

48 pecan halves

16 ounces of semisweet chocolate, divided

1½ cups confectionary dulce de leche

Preheat the oven to 350°F. Line a baking sheet with aluminum foil and coat with nonstick cooking spray. Arrange the pecans in clusters of four, with each one pointing in a different direction like turtle legs, about ½ inch apart. Bake for 7 minutes until golden brown.

Melt 12 ounces of the chocolate in the top of a double boiler and spoon the melted chocolate over the middle of each pecan cluster to form the turtle shells. These are a rustic candy, so don't worry about keeping the turtle perfectly round, but do keep the outer tips of the pecans uncovered to create the look of tiny feet peeking out of the chocolate turtle shell. With the back of a spoon, smooth out the chocolate layer to create an even base and refrigerate on the baking sheet for about 1 hour to set.

When the chocolate is set, add ½ teaspoon of confectionary dulce de leche to the center of each chocolate turtle base. With the back of a spoon, make an oval shape to form the turtle shell.

Melt the remaining 4 ounces of chocolate in the top of the double boiler and transfer to a small, deep bowl. Carefully pick up each turtle by the chocolate base and invert to dip just the dulce de leche dollop into the melted chocolate to cover and set the filling. (Have a dishcloth handy, as your fingertips will get messy with chocolate.) Return the turtle, right side up, to the baking sheet. Dip the remaining turtles and return all to the baking sheet in the same manner. Refrigerate the turtles for another hour to fully set.

The turtles keep, in an airtight container, in the refrigerator for up to 1 week. To serve, return to room temperature so the dulce de leche softens.

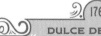

STRAWBERRY NUBE CAKE

This show-stopping layer cake is light as a cloud, hence the name *nube*. As you slice into it, neat rows of ruby-red *frutillas* (strawberries) are revealed. We spend most Easter holidays with friends in Charleston, South Carolina—just in time for strawberry picking season. Barely unpacked, we head to a local farm, get our hands dirty and satisfy our berry *antojos* (cravings) by the bushel, anticipating the first bite of this indulgent cake later that evening for dessert.

FOR THE CAKE

½ pound (2 sticks) unsalted butter, at room temperature

2 cups granulated sugar

4 large eggs

⅓ cup grated orange zest (from about 6 oranges)

3 cups all-purpose flour

1 tablespoon baking powder

¼ teaspoon salt

1 cup whole milk

1 teaspoon pure vanilla extract

2 pounds fresh strawberries

FOR THE FROSTING

1 (8-ounce) container mascarpone cheese, softened

⅔ cup confectionary dulce de leche

⅓ cup granulated sugar

2 cups heavy whipping cream

½ teaspoon pure vanilla bean paste

MAKE THE CAKE: Preheat the oven to 350°F. Butter and flour two 9-by-1½-inch round cake pans. Beat the butter in the bowl of a stand mixer fitted with the paddle attachment until light and fluffy. Gradually add the sugar, beating. With the mixer on medium-low speed, add the egg yolks, one at a time, beating after each addition.

In a large bowl, sift together the flour, baking powder and salt. Add the flour mixture to the batter alternately with the milk, beginning and ending with the flour. Beat at low speed after each addition, just until blended. Stir in the vanilla extract.

In a clean bowl, beat the egg whites at high speed with an electric hand mixer until stiff peaks form. Using a spatula, fold one-third of the egg whites into the batter. Gently fold in the remaining egg whites in two batches. Divide the batter between the prepared cake pans. Bake for 30 minutes, or until a skewer inserted in the center comes out clean. Set the cakes on a wire cooling rack and let cool completely.

PREPARE THE STRAWBERRIES: While the cakes bake, cut a thin slice from the stem end of each of the whole, cleaned strawberries to form a flat base. Set the strawberries aside to dry on a towel.

PREPARE THE FROSTING: In a medium bowl, gently stir together the mascarpone and dulce de leche. Beat the whipping cream and vanilla bean paste with an electric hand mixer at medium speed until foamy; increase the speed to medium-high, and slowly add the sugar, beating until stiff peaks form. Fold one-third of the whipped cream into the mascarpone mixture; gently fold in the remaining whipped cream in 2 batches. Cover the bowl with plastic wrap and refrigerate for at least 30 minutes.

Layer and fill the cake: Place one cooled cake layer on a serving platter and spread the top with ¾ cup of the frosting. Working from the outer edge of the cake toward the center, place the strawberries, pointed tips up, on top of the frosted bottom layer. Spoon 1½ cups frosting into a pastry bag fitted with a large tip (or into a plastic freezer bag with one corner snipped to make a small hole). Pipe the frosting between the strawberries, filling in spaces completely. Gently spread about ¾ cup of the frosting on top of berries.

Carefully place the second cake layer atop the berry layer and generously spread the remaining frosting over the top and sides of the cake. Garnish with the remaining strawberries.

This cake keeps, tightly covered, in the refrigerator for up to 3 days. Cover and allow the frosting to set for 30 minutes before serving.

RUSTIC APPLE CROSTATA

The heavenly taste of this rustic dessert speaks for itself; don't worry about it being neat or pretty. Keep the recipe in mind when apples are in season at your local orchards and farm markets. A hand-formed crostata makes the perfect finish to an autumnal Sunday dinner, perhaps when you've just returned from a pick-your-own spree with a bushel of juicy fresh fruit.

FOR THE DOUGH

2 to 2½ cups unbleached all-purpose flour

1 large egg

1 large egg yolk

1 cup granulated sugar

½ cup unsalted butter

1 to 2 tablespoons 2% or whole milk

FOR THE FILLING

8 to 10 apples (preferably Gala or Fuji), sliced

¼ cup light brown sugar

3 tablespoons unsalted butter

1 tablespoon ground cinnamon

Juice of 1 lemon

1 cup confectionary dulce de leche

FOR THE TOPPING

1 cup old-fashioned oats

¼ cup light brown sugar

2 tablespoons unsalted butter, melted

MAKE THE DOUGH: Put the flour, egg and egg yolk, sugar, butter and milk into a food processor and pulse until the dough forms pea-like lumps. Turn the dough out onto a work surface. With floured hands, gently knead the dough just until moist. Add additional flour or drops of milk as needed for a smooth consistency. Lightly flour the top of the dough and form into a roundish shape. Place it on a small baking sheet and refrigerate, loosely covered with plastic wrap, for 30 minutes.

While the dough chills, preheat the oven to 350°F. Line a baking sheet with parchment paper.

MAKE THE APPLE FILLING: In a large saucepan, combine the apples, brown sugar, butter, cinnamon and lemon juice and cook over medium heat, stirring occasionally, until the apples soften and caramelize.

MAKE THE TOPPING: Put the oats, brown sugar and melted butter in a food processor and pulse just until the mixture is combined and forms a crumble.

On a work surface, roll the chilled dough evenly into a ¼-inch-thick round and transfer to the baking sheet. Spread the dulce de leche on the dough, taking care not to tear it and leaving enough of an edge to fold over, and top with the apple filling. Fold the edge of the pastry over the filling, pleating as necessary, to create a rustic tart. The crostata does not need to be symmetrical, but try not to tear the edges of the dough to keep the filling from leaking. Add the crumble topping to the filling and bake 25 to 30 minutes until golden brown. Transfer the crostata on the baking sheet to a rack and let cool completely.

ITALIAN MERINGUE BROWNIES

Our Argentine friends, Pablo and Julia, serve a version of these decadent brownies at their weekend *asados*. In Argentina, this stunning dessert with its golden-tipped meringue topping is almost as common as s'mores are in the United States, providing that same ambrosial combination of toasted marshmallows and gooey chocolate.

The brownies are quite sweet, so a little goes a long way.

FOR THE BROWNIES

3 sticks plus 2 tablespoons unsalted butter

12 ounces best-quality bittersweet chocolate

6 eggs

1¼ cups superfine sugar

1 tablespoon pure vanilla extract

1½ cups plus 2 tablespoons all-purpose flour

1 teaspoon salt

½ cup white chocolate buttons, chips or morsels

½ cup semisweet chocolate buttons, chips or morsels

TOPPING

1 cup traditional dulce de leche

1 cup superfine sugar

5 egg whites, at room temperature

¼ teaspoon cream of tartar

Preheat the oven to 350°F. Butter a rectangular baking pan (about 9 x 11 inches) and line the bottom with parchment.

Melt the butter and dark chocolate together in a large heavy saucepan over low heat. In a bowl, beat the eggs with the sugar and vanilla. Allow the chocolate mixture to cool a little, then add the egg and sugar mixture and beat well. Fold in flour and salt, and then stir in the white and semisweet chocolate. Beat to combine, then scrape into the baking pan. Bake for 30 to 35 minutes, or until the top is pale brown and speckled, while the center remains dark, dense and gooey. Transfer to a rack to cool.

To prepare the Italian meringue, in a small pot over low heat, combine sugar and ⅓ cup water. Swirl the pot over the burner to dissolve the sugar completely. Increase the heat and boil gently until the syrup is transparent. Remove from the heat and set aside.

In the bowl of an electric mixer, whip eggs whites on low speed until foamy. Add cream of tartar, increase the speed to medium, and beat until soft peaks form. With the mixer running, pour the hot sugar syrup in a thin stream over the whipped egg whites. Beat until the whites are stiff and glossy.

Preheat a broiler. Once the brownies have cooled slightly, poke the top with a fork and generously spread the dulce de leche over so it soaks through. Spoon the meringue over the brownies and broil for 30 seconds to brown the tips. Serve warm, or cover and refrigerate.

DULCE DE LECHE
ICE CREAM PARFAIT

My sister Corina is a great cook. She makes the best chicken *milanesas* (chicken breasts pounded thin, breaded and fried). What she doesn't do is bake, which is why she loves this dessert. It's composed of storebought ingredients that can be prepared right at the dinner table.

4 scoops vanilla ice cream

2 meringue cones (page 173)

Fresh raspberries

Traditional dulce de leche

Whipped cream

Fresh mint

For each serving, put a scoop of vanilla ice cream in a tall footed glass or wine goblet. Top with a layer of dulce de leche. Crumble the meringue shells on top of the dulce de leche and layer with fresh raspberries. Top with fresh whipped cream and garnish with mint.

LEMON POUND CAKE

WITH DULCE DE LECHE GLAZE

I've put an Argentine twist on this traditional lemon buttermilk cake with a dulce de leche glaze. The recipe makes two cakes, or one really large cake if you use a tube pan. I like to make it in smaller loaf pans and freeze one loaf, unglazed, to use later for the trifle on page 183. If you're making one large cake, or both loaf cakes at the same time, double the ingredients for the glaze and use the full amount.

FOR THE CAKE

½ pound (2 sticks) unsalted butter, at room temperature

½ cup original dulce de leche

2 cups granulated sugar

4 extra-large eggs, room temperature

¼ cup grated lemon zest

3 cups all-purpose flour

½ teaspoon baking powder

½ teaspoon baking soda

1 teaspoon salt

¼ cup freshly squeezed lemon juice

¾ cup buttermilk, room temperature

1 teaspoon pure vanilla extract

FOR THE DULCE DE LECHE GLAZE

1 cup confectioners' sugar, sifted

2 tablespoons freshly squeezed lemon juice

1 tablespoon traditional dulce de leche

MAKE THE CAKE: Preheat the oven to 350°F. Butter and flour two 8½-by-4½-by-2½-inch loaf pans and line the bottoms with parchment. In the bowl of a stand mixer fitted with the paddle attachment, cream the butter, dulce de leche and sugar for about 5 minutes, or until light and fluffy. With the mixer on medium speed, beat in eggs one at a time, beating after each addition, and the lemon zest.

In a large bowl, sift together flour, baking powder, baking soda and salt. In another bowl, combine the lemon juice, buttermilk and vanilla. Add the flour and buttermilk mixtures alternately to the batter, beginning and ending with the flour. Divide the batter evenly between the pans, smooth the tops and bake for 45 minutes to 1 hour, or until a skewer inserted in the center comes out clean.

When cakes are done, let cool for 10 minutes then remove from the pans and cool on a wire rack set over a piece of foil.

MAKE THE GLAZE: Combine the confectioners' sugar, lemon and dulce de leche and whisk until smooth. Add a few more drops of juice, if necessary, to create a pourable glaze. Pour over the top of one cake and allow the glaze to dry.

If not eating at once, wrap well and refrigerate. This cake keeps, tightly covered, in the refrigerator for up to 1 week, or at room temperature for 3 days.

DULCE DE LECHE TRIFLE

This is a true last-minute dessert. You can put it together with all homemade ingredients, or run to the store and grab everything you need for more of a semi-homemade version. Either way, people love it. I like to stock all of the ingredients in the fridge, and prepare the trifle tableside so I don't miss any after-dinner banter. I always make sure to double up on the dulce de leche pudding so we have leftovers the following day.

1 cup traditional dulce de leche

2 cups milk

1 (3-ounce) package instant vanilla pudding

3 tablespoons dulce de leche liqueur or Grand Marnier

2 cups cold heavy cream

4 tablespoons confectioners' sugar

1 lemon pound cake (page 182), or a store-bought pound cake

1 pint fresh raspberries

MAKE THE PUDDING: In a medium saucepan over moderate heat, mix the dulce de leche with the milk, whisking until combined. Whisk in the pudding. Bring to a full boil, stirring constantly for 1 minute. Transfer to a bowl and allow to cool; the pudding will thicken as it cools.

ASSEMBLE THE TRIFLE: Cut the pound cake into ¾-inch slices. Place a layer of cake in the bottom of a 2½- to 3-quart glass serving bowl, cutting the pieces to fit. Top with a layer of raspberries and pudding. Repeat the layers of cake, raspberries and pudding, ending with a third layer of cake topped with raspberries.

Whip the cream in a bowl with an electric mixer. When it starts to thicken, add sugar and liqueur and continue to whip until it forms stiff peaks. Decorate the trifle with the whipped cream.

CHOCOLATE SOUFFLÉS

WITH RASPBERRY DULCE DE LECHE SAUCE

I prepare these ahead of time, cover with plastic and store in the refrigerator until after dinner. Before popping them into the oven, I set up a toppings buffet with raspberry sauce, a pot of dulce de leche, freshly whipped cream, raspberries and chopped salted pistachios.

FOR THE SOUFFLÉS

- ¼ cup sugar, plus additional for coating ramekins
- 6 tablespoons (¾ stick) unsalted butter
- 2 tablespoons heavy cream
- 8 ounces best-quality bittersweet chocolate, coarsely chopped
- 4 large egg yolks
- 7 large egg whites
- ¼ teaspoon cream of tartar

FOR THE SAUCE

- 1 package (12 ounces) frozen raspberries in syrup, thawed
- ½ cup seedless raspberry jam
- 3 heaping tablespoons traditional dulce de leche
- 2 tablespoons Chambord or other raspberry liqueur, optional

MAKE THE SOUFFLÉS: Preheat the oven to 375°F. Butter six 1-cup ramekins and coat with sugar. In a small saucepan, melt the butter. Add the cream and bring just to a boil. Remove from the heat and add the chocolate, stirring until smooth. Transfer to a large bowl and stir in the egg yolks.

In another large bowl, using an electric mixer, beat the egg whites with the cream of tartar and a pinch of salt until they just hold stiff peaks. Gradually add ¼ cup sugar, beating until just combined. Stir one-quarter of the whites into chocolate mixture to lighten it, then fold in remaining whites gently but thoroughly.

Divide the soufflé mixture among ramekins and smooth the tops with a knife. Run the tip of a knife around the edges of the soufflés to aid in rising. (Soufflés can be made up to this point one day ahead, then chilled, loosely wrapped in plastic.)

Place the soufflés on a baking sheet in the lower third of the oven and bake until puffed, with cracks in the top and sides, about 20 minutes. Serve immediately with the sauce.

MAKE THE SAUCE: Drain the raspberries, reserving the juice. In a food processor, purée until smooth. Using a spoon, press the purée through a fine-mesh sieve, discarding the seeds.

In a small saucepan over medium heat, cook the jam, 2 tablespoons of the reserved raspberry juices and dulce de leche, whisking constantly. Simmer for 1 minute, then remove from the heat and add the raspberry purée and liqueur, if desired, mixing well. Let cool and serve.

WHITE CHOCOLATE MOUSSE

Chocolate mousse can be served in so many different ways: alone, layered with fruit in parfait fashion or in a trifle. My mom loved white chocolate, and she is the inspiration behind this fluffy dessert. Since almost any fresh fruit may be used, it can be served throughout the year. I like it with whipped cream and strawberries, raspberries or blueberries.

6 ounces high-quality white chocolate, chopped

3 tablespoons unsalted butter

3 large eggs, separated

½ teaspoon cream of tartar

¼ cup confectionary dulce de leche, plus extra for decorating

2 tablespoons sugar

½ cup chilled heavy cream

½ teaspoon pure vanilla extract

Whipped cream and chocolate shavings for garnish

Combine the white chocolate and butter in a heatproof bowl and set it over a pan of boiling water. Stir with a wooden spoon until the chocolate is melted. Remove from the heat and stir in the confectionary dulce de leche until smooth. Don't worry if the dulce de leche begins to separate. Let the mixture cool slightly.

One at a time, add the egg yolks to the white chocolate mixture, using a hand-held mixer to beat until smooth after each addition. Set aside.

In another bowl, beat the egg whites until foamy. Add the cream of tartar and continue beating until soft peaks form. Gradually beat in 1 tablespoon of sugar and continue beating until stiff peaks form. In a separate chilled bowl, beat the heavy cream until it begins to thicken. Add the remaining 1 tablespoon of sugar and vanilla, and continue beating until the cream holds soft peaks.

To assemble, gently fold the beaten egg whites into the chocolate mixture and then fold in the whipped cream. Take care to not overwork the mousse or it will be heavy. Divide among stemmed glasses. Cover and chill for several hours. Garnish with whipped cream and chocolate shavings before serving.

DULCE DE LECHE FONDUE

This is a breeze to make. Use your imagination when assembling the bite-sized dipping foods. I tend to combine several different fruits and I love angel food cake, as it holds up to the velvety rich fondue for dipping, but you could certainly use pretzels or other salty snacks for a sweet-and-salty experience.

For the fondue, I follow the dark chocolate dulce de leche recipe. If you have original dulce de leche on hand, add 2 ounces of good quality dark chocolate for an extra depth of flavor, or forego the chocolate altogether and focus on the golden color. Just make sure that the fondue doesn't boil, as it can begin to caramelize.

3 cups dark chocolate dulce de leche

1 cup milk or ½ cup cherry brandy or kirsch

2 ounces semisweet chocolate

1 cinnamon stick

Warm the milk over moderately low heat with the cinnamon stick. Once it's hot, add the dark chocolate dulce de leche, stirring often to obtain a silky smooth consistency. Reduce the heat to a simmer.

Arrange an assortment of bite-sized dipping foods on a lazy Susan around a fondue pot. Serve with chunks of angel food cake, cubed apples, pears, bananas and strawberries. Spear with fondue forks or wooden skewers, dip, swirl and enjoy!

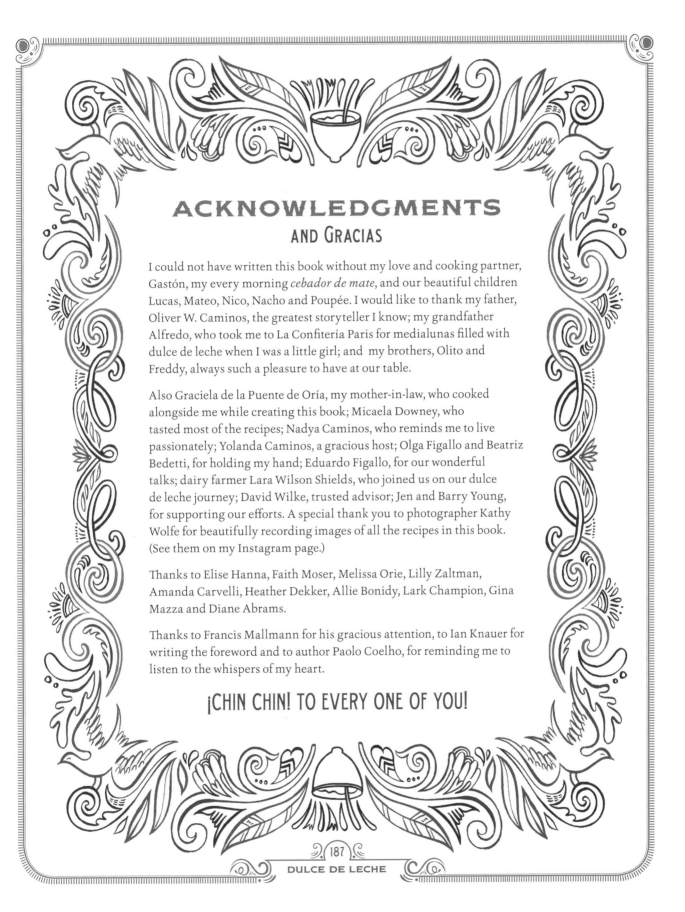

ACKNOWLEDGMENTS
AND GRACIAS

I could not have written this book without my love and cooking partner, Gastón, my every morning *cebador de mate*, and our beautiful children Lucas, Mateo, Nico, Nacho and Poupée. I would like to thank my father, Oliver W. Caminos, the greatest storyteller I know; my grandfather Alfredo, who took me to La Confitería Paris for medialunas filled with dulce de leche when I was a little girl; and my brothers, Olito and Freddy, always such a pleasure to have at our table.

Also Graciela de la Puente de Oría, my mother-in-law, who cooked alongside me while creating this book; Micaela Downey, who tasted most of the recipes; Nadya Caminos, who reminds me to live passionately; Yolanda Caminos, a gracious host; Olga Figallo and Beatriz Bedetti, for holding my hand; Eduardo Figallo, for our wonderful talks; dairy farmer Lara Wilson Shields, who joined us on our dulce de leche journey; David Wilke, trusted advisor; Jen and Barry Young, for supporting our efforts. A special thank you to photographer Kathy Wolfe for beautifully recording images of all the recipes in this book. (See them on my Instagram page.)

Thanks to Elise Hanna, Faith Moser, Melissa Orie, Lilly Zaltman, Amanda Carvelli, Heather Dekker, Allie Bonidy, Lark Champion, Gina Mazza and Diane Abrams.

Thanks to Francis Mallmann for his gracious attention, to Ian Knauer for writing the foreword and to author Paolo Coelho, for reminding me to listen to the whispers of my heart.

¡CHIN CHIN! TO EVERY ONE OF YOU!

INDEX

ABOUT THE AUTHOR

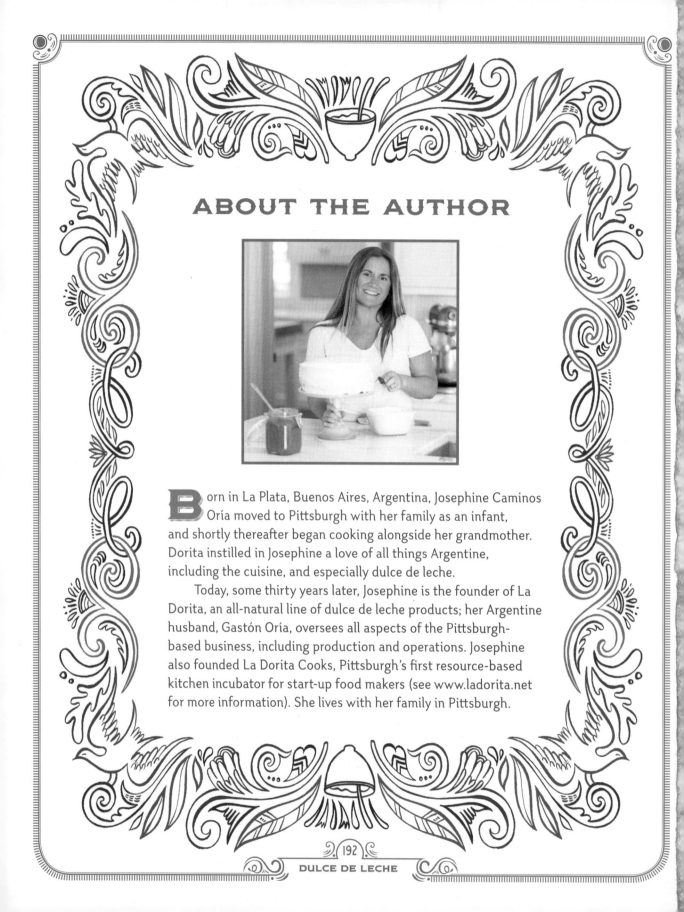

Born in La Plata, Buenos Aires, Argentina, Josephine Caminos Oría moved to Pittsburgh with her family as an infant, and shortly thereafter began cooking alongside her grandmother. Dorita instilled in Josephine a love of all things Argentine, including the cuisine, and especially dulce de leche.

Today, some thirty years later, Josephine is the founder of La Dorita, an all-natural line of dulce de leche products; her Argentine husband, Gastón Oría, oversees all aspects of the Pittsburgh-based business, including production and operations. Josephine also founded La Dorita Cooks, Pittsburgh's first resource-based kitchen incubator for start-up food makers (see www.ladorita.net for more information). She lives with her family in Pittsburgh.